Be Careful
What You Pray For...

When I left the pastorate in 1975 to enter the itinerant ministry, Kaye and I agreed we would never turn down an invitation because of finances. It wasn't long before I had to put my money where my mouth was.

We were invited to participate in a "mission" conference. Kaye and I both felt strongly that God wanted us to be a part of this meeting, but we figured our total cost would be close to $1000 — about $990 more than we had. We decided to accept the invitation anyway, making the money a matter of prayer and faith.

Several months passed. It was Friday, and we were scheduled to leave the next day for the conference. Still, the money was not there. We had been shopping that morning and pulled into the driveway around noon. I went through the gate in our fence, and on my way to the back door I stumbled over something. At my feet I saw some strange white canvas bags stacked neatly on the doorstep. Printed on the bag were these words: DENVER MINT, $50, 1975 Penny.

I quickly counted the bags — twenty! That's $1000 in pennies. I didn't know where they had come from, but I had to do something with them fast. In the lower right-hand corner of the bag was the name of a local bank.

"Southwest Bank. May I help you?"

"Uh, hello. Uh, listen, are, uh, are you missing any pennies?"

"Beg your pardon?"

Eventually I was connected to someone else to whom I told my tale and she said that although she did not know of any missing pennies, since their name was on the sacks she would send someone out to pick them up.

"No, don't do that," I said suddenly, a light dawning. "I think I know where they came from."

Logic. The pennies were on my doorstep. Stacked deliberately with loving care. One thousand dollars. My money. My prayer.

I have this weird friend. Several weeks before, I had complained to him about having to pay a bill I didn't think I owed and that I had a good mind to pay it in cash — with pennies. In the meantime, my friend, who didn't know about my $1000 need, sold some property and decided to make a $1000 gift to my ministry. Remembering my remark about paying a bill with pennies, he made elaborate plans with the local bank to have $1000 in pennies shipped down from the Denver mint.

And that's how they got to me. It's like they say, be careful what you pray for . . . God just might answer it. In our case, God didn't just answer our prayer — He did it with a flourish.

When you're looking for a miracle . . .

DON'T JUST STAND THERE
Pray
SOMETHING

Ronald Dunn

THOMAS NELSON
Since 1798

For other products and live events,
visit us at: thomasnelson.com

Published in Nashville, Tennessee, by Thomas Nelson, Inc.

Unless otherwise indicated, Scripture quotations are from the NEW KING JAMES VERSION of the Bible. Copyright © 1979, 1980, 1982, Thomas Nelson, Inc., Publishers.
Scripture quotations designated NIV are from The Holy Bible: New International Version, © 1973, 1978, 1984 by the International Bible Society. Published by Zondervan Bible Publishers, Grand Rapids Michigan.
Scripture quotations designated NAS are from the New American Standard Bible, The Lockman Foundation © 1960, 1962, 1963, 1968, 1971, 1975, 1977.
Scripture quotations designated Williams are from The New Testament in the Language of the People, translated by Charles B. Williams, © 1937 Edith S. Williams, published by Holman Bible Publishers, Nashville, Tennessee.

Library of Congress Cataloging-in-Publication Data

Dunn, Ronald.
    Don't just stand there pray something / Ronald Dunn.
        p. cm.
    At head of title: When you're looking for a miracle.
    Originally published: San Bernardino : Here's Life Publishers, © 1991.
    Includes bibliographical references.
    ISBN 0-8407-4393-9 (pbk.)
    1. Intercessory prayer — Christianity. 2. Spiritual life — Baptist authors. I. Title.
BV215.D84 1992   92-40879
248.3'2 — DC20   CIP

31 QWE 06

To my father

Cecil Dunn

and to the memory of my mother

Eunice Bridges Dunn

Contents

PART THREE: The Life That Prays

PART FOUR: The God Who Hears

Acknowledgments

Some acknowledgments are in order:

Joanne Gardner, my secretary since 1966, spent many long hours transcribing tapes.

I'm indebted to those precious intercessors of MacArthur Blvd. Baptist Church who, with me, learned how to get bread for hungry travelers.

My thanks to Dan Benson for making me write a better book.

I'm grateful to my son Stephen and my daughter Kimberly for their permission, permission I'm sure they would have given had I asked (it's easier to get forgiveness than permission), to drag them in as illustrations.

I'm indebted to Stephen for his help in gathering and organizing material.

And, as always, to my wife Kaye for her uncountable kindnesses and her unaccountable love and for reading and rereading the manuscript with a loving but lethal eye that tries to keep my writing honest.

In the Beginning

In 1972 the church I pastored launched a 24-hour, seven-day-a-week intercessory prayer ministry. God had been awakening us to prayer for some time. Throughout the week clusters of people were gathering to pray during lunch hours or early evenings. I had preached for three months on intercessory praying, and it was all climaxed by the inauguration of our prayer ministry. We did not organize to create a prayer ministry—we organized a ministry already created.

The intercessory prayer ministry revolutionized the lives of many who were prayed for, and, I believe, the lives of those who did the praying.

Of course, there had to be a book. I finished the first draft in 1973—and laid it aside for fifteen years.

Then followed some years of living dangerously, of crises in which everything I preached was challenged. I found that what I had preached was true—I had just preached it too easily. I'm glad I waited until now to finish the book.

PART ONE

God's
Great Idea

Just
Do It

Prayer is . . .

No, no. Start over.

Prayer is . . .

Come on, concentrate!

Prayer is . . .

Excuse me—I'm having a hard time keeping a proper image of prayer in my mind. Do you know the picture I get when I think about prayer? I've had this since I was a kid. The scene is a little Spanish mission in the desert. Standing in front of it is a monk with a tonsured haircut, wearing a coarse brown robe (it looks hot and makes me itch) girded with a length of rope. His hands are clasped prayerfully in front of him; he appears meek and fragile, unworldly, unsophisticated, and undernourished (from fasting, probably). He stands there gazing up at the Lone Ranger and Tonto, their steeds straining at the reins with flared nostrils snorting and legs dancing amid exploding clouds of dust. The Lone Ranger and Tonto (pure in heart, hence unafraid) have drawn their guns, and their faces are fixed in grim determination.

The monk says something about going with them.

"You are a brave man, Father," the masked man says, "but it may be dangerous. You had better stay here where it's safe."

"But I want to help," the monk says.

The strong yet kind eyes of the masked man fasten on the man of God. "You can pray."

Suddenly the great white horse rears up on its hind legs, and with a wave of his hat and a hearty "Heigh Ho Silver—Awa-a-a-ay!" the Lone Ranger and his faithful companion gallop off to the danger that awaits them.

The camera of my imagination does not follow the priest into the mission to watch him pray. It chases after the Lone Ranger and Tonto. That's where the action is.

Prayer's Poor Image

Let's face it. In spite of all the reverence that surrounds it, prayer suffers from a poor image. Some people dismiss prayer as a weak alternative to practical action, an alibi for doing nothing. Offering to pray for someone is often nothing but a graceful way to excuse ourselves from an awkward situation; it is an exit line. Prayer is something the women do (especially during

World Missions Week), something for the more delicate saints to engage in while those who get the job done are out getting the job done.

I remember addressing a group of church leaders in Honolulu. They had invited me to speak specifically on prayer and how to develop an intercessory prayer ministry in the local church. I pointed out to them that the church had programs for just about everything else — witnessing programs, discipleship programs, stewardship programs — but few churches had a prayer program. This seemed ironic considering the great emphasis the Bible places on prayer.

After a morning session, one of the delegates, a director of a denominational evangelism department, tapped me on the shoulder, gave me a conspiratorial wink and drew me aside.

"You know," he whispered, "I think this prayer thing is a great idea, but I'm afraid it might get out of hand."

"What do you mean?"

"Well," he said. "People could get so caught up in praying they wouldn't do anything."

He didn't say, "anything *else*." He said, "anything," period. When I realized the man was serious, I assured him I had yet to come across a church that was praying so much they had to be told to slack off. We would just have to cross that bridge when we came to it. So far, I haven't seen anything resembling that bridge.

Prayer is not a substitute for work, or merely preparation for work. It *is* work.

That is the other side of prayer's bad image—the image of ancient saints kneeling on hard cold floors in the dark hours of winter mornings, crying long to the Lord. Prayer is serious business, they say to us; there is no room for foolishness here. To do it right demands rigorous discipline.

The Most Intimidating Word in the Bible

Its seriousness makes prayer one of the most intimidating words in the Christian vocabulary. We've all been daunted by the pronouncements of old divines like Martin Luther, who said, "I have so much to do today that I shall spend the first three hours in prayer," and the stories of prayer warriors like Praying Hyde of India, or David Brainerd who prayed in knee-deep snow so long and so vigorously the snow around him melted, and he caught pneumonia and died. Not to forget old "Camel-Knees," the apostle James who, according to tradition, spent so much time praying his knees resembled the calloused knees of a camel.

The hallowed ghosts of these ancestors have dumped piles of guilt on all of us. I suspect most of us have had a go at the 4 A.M. ritual—rising a great while before day to "wrestle in prayer."

"No pain, no gain," seems to be the motto of prayer. I've never really understood why prayer must be a test of physical endurance. I much prefer the prayer lunch to the prayer breakfast.

So we knock any talk about prayer being work, or requiring personal sacrifice, blood, sweat and tears—but only when we say it about prayer. Sacrifice, pain and hard work are admired in a 26-mile marathon for muscular dystrophy. In prayer they are ridiculed.

That was my mental picture of prayer (was it yours, too?) until I discovered something important, something that changed my whole idea about prayer (will it change yours, too?).

I discovered that prayer is not a religious exercise—it is a human necessity.

In one way or another, to one god or another, we humans have always prayed, whether we called it that or not. We are devoured by the need of something outside ourselves, something beyond our reach, something spiritual or supernatural, a place to run to, to feel, however slightly, that there is someone out there to cry to, someone who takes notice of our predicament. We long to escape the sense of crushing fate, the feeling that all things are fixed and unalterable. Yes, prayer is much more than a religious exercise. It is a human necessity.

The Christian's Secret Weapon

Prayer means that I never have to say, "There's nothing I can do." I can always do something, something great, as great as Jesus did. Even greater. I don't have to just stand there—I can pray something.

I discovered that prayer is the secret weapon of the kingdom of God. It is like a missile that can be fired toward any spot on earth, travel undetected at the speed of thought, and hit its target every time.

It can even be armed with a delayed detonation device. In His prayer of John 17, Jesus said, "I do not pray for these alone, but also for those who will believe in Me through their word (John 17:20). His prayer

spans the centuries and embraces all who have believed,
or who ever will believe. Every time someone turns to
Christ, the prayer of Jesus is answered again—two
thousand years old and still being answered.

The implications are staggering. We, too, can
pray about things yet to happen, things, for instance,
in the lives of our children—and their children. We can
wrap them in the arms of intercession and march them
through the fires of hell and into the gates of heaven.
This is the inheritance we can leave our children—an
inheritance of prayer, prayers lifted to God long before
the children were born, prayers answered long after we
are gone.

There's more. Satan has no defense against this
weapon; he does not have an anti-prayer missile. For
instance, the unbeliever has many defenses against our
evangelistic efforts. He can refuse to attend church, and
if he does occasionally show up, he can shift into neutral
and count the cracks in the ceiling. You can go to his
home, but he doesn't have to let you in. Hand him a
tract on the street, and he can throw it away. Get on
TV, and he can switch channels. Call him on the phone,
and he can hang up. But he cannot prevent the Lord
Jesus from knocking at the door of his heart in response
to our intercession. People we cannot reach any other
way can be reached by way of the throne of grace.

We Can Do Something—Now!

We do not pray by default—because there's
nothing else we can do. We pray because it is the best
thing we can do. We don't have to just stand there—we
can pray something. Like this mother of a teenager did.

I was speaking at a banquet for a church's intercessory prayer ministry when she shared a recent answer to prayer. A few days before, as she was getting a pie ready to put into the oven, the phone rang. It was the school nurse: Her son had come down with a high fever and would she come and take him home?

The mother calculated how long it would take to drive to school and back, and how long the pie should bake, and concluded there was enough time. Popping the pie in the oven, she left for school. When she arrived, her son's fever was worse and the nurse urged her to take him to the doctor.

Seeing her son like that—his face flushed, his body trembling and dripping with perspiration—frayed her, and she drove to the clinic as fast as she dared. She was frayed a bit more waiting for the doctor to emerge from the examination room, which he was now doing, walking toward her with a slip of paper in his hand.

"Get him to bed," he told her, handing her the prescription, "and start him on this right away."

By the time she got the boy home and in bed and headed out again for the shopping mall, she was not only frayed, but frazzled and frantic as well. And she had forgotten about the pie in the oven. At the mall she found a pharmacy, got the prescription filled and rushed back to the car.

Which was locked.

Yes, there were her keys, hanging in the ignition switch, locked inside the car. She ran back into the mall, found a phone and called home. When her son finally answered, she blurted out, "I've locked the keys inside the car!"

The boy was barely able to speak. In a hoarse voice he whispered, "Get a wire coat hanger, Mom. You can get in with that." The phone went dead.

She began searching the mall for a wire coat hanger—which turned out not to be easy. Wooden hangers and plastic hangers were there in abundance, but shops didn't use wire hangers anymore. After combing through a dozen stores, she found one that was behind the times just enough to use wire hangers.

Hurrying out of the mall, she allowed herself a smile of relief. As she was about to step off the curb, she halted. She stared at the wire coat hanger.

"I don't know what to do with this!"

Then she remembered the pie in the oven. All the frustrations of the past hour collapsed on her and she began crying. Then she prayed. "Dear Lord, my boy is sick and he needs this medicine and my pie is in the oven and the keys are locked in the car and, Lord, I don't know what to do with this coat hanger. Dear Lord, send somebody who does know what to do with it, and I really need that person NOW, Lord. Amen."

She was wiping her eyes when a beat-up old car pulled up to the curb and stopped in front of her. A young man, twentyish-looking, in a T-shirt and ragged jeans, got out. The first thing she noticed about him was the long, stringy hair, and then the beard that hid everything south of his nose. He was coming her way. When he drew near she stepped in front of him and held out the wire coat hanger. "Young man," she said, "do you know how to get into a locked car with one of these?"

He gaped at her for a moment, then plucked the hanger from her hand. "Where's the car?"

Telling the story that night, she said she had never seen anything like it—it was simply amazing how easily he got into her car. A quick look at the door and window, a couple of twists of the coat hanger and bam! Just like that, the door was open.

When she saw the door open she threw her arms around him. "Oh," she said, "the Lord sent you! You're such a good boy. You must be a Christian."

He stepped back and said, "No ma'am, I'm not a Christian, and I'm not a good boy. I just got out of prison yesterday."

She jumped at him and she hugged him again— fiercely. "Bless God!" she cried. "He sent me a professional!"

She hadn't just stood there—she'd prayed something.

That woman had a great prayer-image. She did exactly what Jesus said she should do in Luke 18:1— that "men always ought to pray and not lose heart."

Fighting City Hall

To punctuate these words, Jesus told a parable. It's the story of an unjust judge who doesn't fear God and doesn't have much use for people either, and an unfortunate widow who comes to him seeking justice.

In the ancient world, before Social Security and Medicare and other charitable programs, a widow was the most helpless of all creatures. When her husband died she lost her provider and her protector and was thrown on the mercy of society, of which there was little to be thrown upon. A widow was the symbol of all who were poor and defenseless, and when Jesus picked a widow for the starring role in this drama He was emphasizing in the strongest way possible the weakness and helplessness of the person.

Now let's pause here for a minute. Stop thinking of this parable as an old, musty, out-of-date fable recorded in some ancient tome. This is right now. Here is one person, the most destitute of people, shut out, alienated, alone, assaulting the irresistible, destiny-determining powers of life, demanding justice. This woman is fighting city hall.

Sound familiar? It's a story we all know only too well, isn't it?

As a matter of fact, it could be the story of every one of us. Life is tough and we often find ourselves struggling against the odds to squeeze a little justice out of an unjust world.

But we can do more than wring our hands in despair. We can do what this widow did—we can pray. Will praying really make a difference? Well, let's see if it made a difference in the widow's case.

Remember, she has no influence, no money, nothing to make it worthwhile to the judge to vindicate her, but she is relentless in her pursuit. Finally the judge says:

> Though I do not fear God nor regard man, yet because this widow troubles me I will avenge her, lest by her continual coming she weary me (Luke 18:4,5).

The meaning is obvious: We ought always to pray and not lose heart. Here's why:

> Hear what the unjust judge said. And shall God not avenge His own elect who cry out day and

night to Him, though He bears long with them?
(verses 6,7)

Jesus is not comparing God to the unjust judge,
He is *contrasting* the two. He is arguing from the lesser
to the greater. In other words, the meaner the judge,
the better our God. If this sorry clod of injustice will
grant the request of a troublesome widow, how much
more will the heavenly Judge, perfect in love and righteousness, hear our cry and vindicate our cause?

Then Jesus rams home the question: "Nevertheless, when the Son of Man comes, will He really find
faith on the earth?" (Luke 18:8). The construction of
the question implies a negative answer: Not likely.

But it is a certain kind of faith Jesus will be
looking for when He returns. In the Greek text, *faith*
carries a definite article that points to a specific kind of
faith, literally, *"this* kind of faith." When Jesus returns,
will He find on earth the kind of faith that prays without
ceasing, faith like that of the widow who refused to lose
heart and by her "continual coming" seized the prize?

If this book were a sermon I would choose as my
text Ezekiel 22:30 :

> So I sought for a man among them who would
> make up a wall, and stand in the gap before Me
> on behalf of the land, that I should not destroy
> it; but I found no one.

God has always sought intercessors, someone to
stand in the gap before Him for the sake of the land,
but He has a hard time finding them. In Ezekiel's day
God looked for a man to stand in the breech that sin
had made between God and Israel. He found no one.
Isaiah tells us that God looked for a man, but found no

one and "wondered that there was no intercessor"
(Isaiah 59:16).

God is still looking, and when Jesus returns He
will still be looking for an intercessor, someone with
"that kind of faith." I write this book with the hope that
when He returns He will find you and me "standing in
the gap." Doing something. Praying.

People
Just Like Us

I know what some of you are thinking. You're
thinking: *Sure, it's easy for this guy to talk about prayer.
He's got it all together, just like all the other people who
write books on happy marriages and successful parent-
ing and winning self-images.*

It's amazing how we romanticize "celebrities."
The great American pastime—idolizing movie stars,
singers, athletes. "We fawn over them, poring over the
minutiae of their lives: the clothes they wear, the food
they eat, the aerobic routines they follow, the people
they love, the toothpaste they use."[1]

Christians do the same with religious authors
and speakers. It's almost impossible not to. Look at the
book, new and shiny, the dust cover ablaze with promises; smell the excitement and the ink. On the back, in
full color, you find the author's picture with his arm

around his/her mate (who is also an author and popular
speaker), leaning against a split-rail fence in front of a
rambling country home. The happy, smiling faces of
these two people show they have it all together—and
their children: two sons, one a doctor, the other a
lawyer; two daughters (the youngest a former Miss
Peach Festival), both married to dynamic, young ministers.

After the closing service of a Bible conference
one woman came up to me to tell me how much the week
had meant to her. Then she stepped back, clasped her
hands to her chest, tilted her head, and with a wistful
look in her eyes, said "Oh, you have such a beautiful
wife; you make such a beautiful couple—your whole life
is just beautiful!"

I guess I should have told her about the argument my wife and I had had that morning. It probably
would have encouraged her more than all my sermons.

Listen, I know many of the people who write the
books and make the videos, and I've got news for you.
They're not doing any better than you are!

They have their fair share of family woes and
marital distress; they weep over rebellious children;
they worry about money; they spend sleepless nights
battling fear and anxiety. They know what it means to
be sucked into the black pit of depression. They are
acquainted with grief and sorrow.

What I'm trying to say is, these people aren't
sitting around waiting for a vacancy in the Trinity; they
are not spiritual experts who have found the secret and
are now letting us in on it. They are fellow pilgrims
sharing what they have seen along the way; they are

digging wells in the desert for those who come after them. They are people just like you and me.

The "Star" System

They say it was the "star" system that killed Hollywood. That same star system has just about done in the church. Every church has its stars, those with obvious popular talents and gifts. These few have become the performers and the rest of us have become the audience.

Philip Yancey writes about the star/servant syndrome.

> Maybe one problem underlying the scandal of Christian superstars is that we distort the kingdom of God by training our spotlight not on the servants, but on the stars.

Then he quotes Henri Nouwen:

> Keep your eyes on the one who refuses to turn stones into bread, jump from great heights or rule with great temporal power. Keep your eyes on the one who says, "Blessed are the poor, the gentle, those who mourn and those who hunger and thirst for righteousness; blessed are the merciful, the peacemakers and those who are persecuted in the cause of uprighteousness."[2]

Blessed are people just like us.

I remember the words of D. Martyn Lloyd-Jones concerning prayer:

> I have always hesitated to deal with this subject. I have preached on prayer when it has come in a passage through which I have been working; but I have never presumed to produce a book on prayer, or even a booklet.[3]

Which, I suppose, proves the saying, "Fools rush in where wise men never go." Yet that is precisely the attitude that frightens us away from prayer. We're afraid to touch it. Prayer is not untouchable. God did not mean for us to hold it in that kind of awe.

Prayer was God's idea. He created it for people who are weakened by sin, fickle in their commitment, at times overwhelmed by doubt, often discouraged and bewildered, and nearly always fretting about life.

That's a good description of the disciples. None of us would call them supersaints, and yet the most significant words Jesus ever spoke concerning prayer, He spoke to His disciples—men who only a few hours later, every last one of them, abandoned their Master. These men were scared to death to be left on their own.

During His last hours with them before the cross, Jesus promised, "I will not leave you helpless orphans" (John 14:18, WILLIAMS). That was exactly what they were afraid of—being left like helpless orphans. They couldn't bear the thought that He might leave them, which lately He had being talking about a lot. Every time Jesus brought up the cross, they tried to change the subject. They must have thought, *We've been such a failure with Him, what will we be without Him?* People just like us.

"Ah, but Peter," you say, "he wasn't afraid." No, he wasn't—but he should have been. It is significant that the one disciple who thought he had it all together is the one who made the loudest flop. In this business, your fear and trembling are not weaknesses; rather, they are advantages.

What did Jesus say to people like us? The last words of a great leader are always deemed significant,

so what were Jesus' last words? What was their significance?

Eavesdropping on Jesus

Let's join the disciples on that last night Jesus
spent with them before the cross and see if we can
overhear their conversation.

It's around midnight, and they are coming from
the upper room where they celebrated the Passover. We
fall in behind the small band as Jesus leads them
through the streets of Jerusalem and out the Eastern
Gate. We wonder where He is going. Oh yes, He's
crossing the Kedron. Of course. He is bringing us to one
of His favorite hideaways, the Garden of Gethsemane
at the foot of Mount Olivet.

As we walk, Jesus continues the ominous discourse He began in the upper room. The pale moonlight
reveals the bewildered looks on the men's faces. The
men shuffle close together, straining to hear every
word. It has been an unsettling evening. They are
perplexed by the strange behavior of their fellow disciple, Judas, and the cryptic conversation that had
passed between him and Jesus.

Jesus is speaking in riddles—and we are one
with the disciples in their confusion. Now Jesus says
something about leaving us and something about His
Father's house.

One of the disciples speaks. It sounds like Philip.
"Lord, show us the Father, and it is sufficient for us"
(John 14:8).

*Good question, Philip! That's what we need—a
more definite word, and unquestionable vision. Let us*

*see not by faith only, but by sight, too. That will be
enough, even if He does leave us.*

Jesus answers:

> He who has seen Me has seen the Father . . . Do
> you not believe that I am in the Father, and the
> Father in Me? The words that I say to you I do
> not speak on My own authority; but the Father
> who dwells in me does the works. Believe Me
> that I am in the Father and the Father in Me,
> or else believe Me for the sake of the works
> themselves (John 14:9-11).

Philip had said "Show us the Father," as though
he had never seen Him, but Jesus insists he has seen
Him. He just didn't know it. Every time he watched
Jesus heal a leper, he saw the Father. Every time he
listened to Jesus teach, he was hearing the Father.

Right now the disciples don't understand, but
later they will realize that with these words Jesus
revealed the secret of His life and work, and it would
soon be the secret of their life and work as well.

The Jesus Secret

By His answer Jesus was saying, "I am not the
source of My own sufficiency. The things I said and
did—they did not initiate with Me. It was the Father."

Jesus disclaimed any credit for the words He
spoke or the works He performed. This helps us understand what He meant when He said,

> Most assuredly, I say to you, the Son can do
> nothing of Himself, but what He sees the
> Father do; for whatever He does, the Son
> also does in like manner (John 5:19).

And again in verse 30:

> I can of Myself do nothing. As I hear, I judge;
> and My judgment is righteous, because I do not
> seek My own will but the will of the Father who
> sent Me.

The secret surfaces again in John 8:28:

> Then Jesus said to them, "When you lift up the
> Son of Man, then you will know that I am He,
> and that I do nothing of Myself; but as My
> Father taught Me, I speak these things."

And again:

> For I have not spoken on My own authority;
> but the Father who sent Me gave Me a com-
> mand, what I should say and what I should
> speak (John 12:49).

The explanation of the miracles Jesus worked and the words He spoke lies with the Father. He did those things — through Jesus — but He did them.

"Listen to Me, Philip. The secret of the works is not My physical *presence*. And if the secret is not My physical *presence*, then My physical *absence* won't make any difference.

"As a matter of fact, if you will trust Me, the works that I have done, you will continue to do, and you will even do greater works than I have done.

"You think My leaving will end My work and make everything difficult for you. But My elevation to the right hand of the Father will enable you to do through My intercession greater works than I have done. My presence in heaven and the Spirit's presence in you is the pledge of even greater power and greater works."

The Lord is leaving, but His departure won't dismantle His work.

A Fantastic Promise

Then Jesus makes an extraordinary promise to the disciples — and to us.

> Most assuredly, I say to you, he who believes in Me, the works that I do he will do also; and greater works than these he will do, because I go to My Father (John 14:12).

I say "and us" because the promise is to him who "believes in Me," and that's us.

To those who believe in Him, Jesus promises two things: **one**, they will *equal* His works, and, **two**, they will *exceed* His works. Fifty days after He made that promise, in the very city where He was crucified, the disciples did equal and exceed His works. After ten days in the upper room, the disciples emerged with the power of the Holy Spirit within them, and after a short sermon by Peter, three thousand people were added to the fledgling church.

For as long as I can remember, we've been trying to do it again, but the Pentecostal power continues to elude us. I don't know many Christians who would say that the church is living up to the promise of John 14:12. So the question is, why not?

To answer that question we must first understand what Jesus meant by *greater works*.

Perhaps the real key is found in the phrase we often overlook: "because I go to My Father." Jesus makes it clear that the promise of greater works can be fulfilled only if He returns to the Father. Why? Why was it necessary for Him to ascend to heaven before the disciples could realize this promise? The ascension certainly was not essential to the working of physical miracles. They had been doing that for three years.

Jesus is evidently speaking of something different, something on a higher level, something in a new dimension.

Upon ascending, Jesus would send the Spirit (John 7:39; 16:7). Jesus Himself would occupy the place of intercession to hear and answer the prayers of His disciples (who were people just like us, remember). It was this that would make possible the doing of greater works.

Jesus is emphasizing the union that will exist between Him and His disciples although they will be separated physically. He is going away but He will remain with them and the work He started will continue and even increase. His physical absence will not diminish the work—it will enhance it. Barnabas Lindars says, "As their works are the works of Jesus, they will be just as much the activity of God in the world as His own works were."[4]

"Works" and "greater works" refer not so much to the independent and specific acts of the disciples, but rather to the fact that everything they do will actually be done by Jesus through them.

In the Hands of a Champion

I used to play tennis quite a lot. I wasn't very good, but I was always open to anything that could help me. One day I was watching a match on TV, and I saw a commercial advertising the Wilson T-2000 metal racquet. It showed Jimmy Connors making a lot of fancy shots while a hidden narrator said, "The Wilson T-

2000. The only metal racquet ever to win both Wimbledon and Forest Hills."

So that was my problem! All this time I had played with a wooden Dunlop Maxply. If the Wilson T-2000 could win Wimbledon and Forest Hills, it could certainly handle my little matches.

Well, I played with one all that summer. And I lost all summer. That racquet didn't do anything for me. I concluded that the Wilson Sporting Goods Company was guilty of false advertising.

The truth is, the Wilson T-2000 didn't win Wimbledon or Forest Hills. Jimmy Connors did — using the Wilson T-2000. When the fans walked away from the match that day they didn't talk about what a great racquet the Wilson T-2000 was; they talked about what a great player Jimmy Connors was. And I'm sure the prize check was made out to Jimmy Connors and not to you-know-who.

Now in tennis, a racquet is essential — but it isn't the racquet that wins. It's the champion who wins, using the racquet. In the doing of works and greater works, Jesus is the champion and we are the racquet in His hands.

The "going" of Jesus meant the "greater works" of the disciples. His ascension meant the descent of the empowering Spirit and the inauguration of Christ's heavenly intercession, thus enabling the church to fulfill its mission of evangelizing the world. J. C. Ryle points out:

> Greater works mean more conversions. There is no greater work possible than the conversion of a soul.[5]

What Jesus means we may see in the narratives of the Acts. There are few miracles of healing, but the emphasis is on the mighty works of conversion. On the day of Pentecost alone more believers were added to the little band of believers than throughout Christ's entire earthly life. There we see a literal fulfillment of "greater works than these shall be done." During His lifetime the Son of God was confined in His influence to a comparatively small sector of Palestine. After His departure His followers were able to work in widely scattered places and influence much larger numbers of men.[6]

Which brings us back to the question of why most of the church is not living up to the promise of greater works.

The best place to find the answer is in the promise itself. How did Jesus intend us to realize the fulfillment of that promise? The pledge of greater works in John 14:12 is followed by another promise in verse 13: "And whatever you ask in My name, that will I do, that the Father may be glorified in the Son."

Our Model Verse

Notice that verse 13 starts with "And." When I was a young preacher I was told, "Never take as a complete text any verse that starts with 'and' because it isn't complete."

Instead of stopping at verse 12, we should move right into verse 13: "And greater works than these he will do, because I go to My Father [verse 12]. *And* whatever you ask in My name that I will do" (verse 13).

The greater works of verse 12 are accomplished by the praying of verse 13. Verse 13 becomes our model verse.

The book of Acts is filled with prayer meetings; every forward thrust the first church made was immersed in prayer. Take another look at the church at Pentecost. They prayed ten days and preached ten minutes and three thousand people were saved. Today we pray ten minutes and preach ten days and are ecstatic if anyone is saved.

But remember, Jesus said we would do it the way He did it; His secret would become our secret. Did Jesus pray? Was it a conspicuous part of His life? If Jesus could say and do only what He heard and saw the Father do, He had to spend a lot of time listening and seeing. And He did. There was a recognizable rhythm in the life of Jesus: He would withdraw to meditate, then go out to minister. Again and again this pattern repeated itself. The public life of Jesus was supported by His private life with His Father.

A number of years ago, the late Alan Redpath, former pastor of Moody Memorial Church in Chicago and a man greatly used of God around the world, suffered a severe stroke. Afterward while he was convalescing, he said, "I believe the Lord has taught me this lesson above all: *Never undertake more Christian work than can be covered in believing prayer.* Each of us has to work out what this means in personal experience in relation to our ministry, but I believe it is an abiding principle for us all. To fail here is to act not in faith but in presumption."[7]

I remember the first request that came to our prayer chapel. After a fourteen-week blitzkrieg of preaching on intercessory prayer, we signed up two hundred excited intercessors and our beautiful prayer chapel was at last ready.

The phone rang, signaling the inaugural petition. We were in business. It was one of our mothers — a terrified mother, calling from the hospital where they had just brought her two-year-old son. Somehow the little boy had gotten hold of a can of automotive engine cleaner, worked the cap off and drank some of the toxic liquid. He was screaming and convulsing when they rushed him into the emergency room.

The doctor offered no hope that the boy would survive. He had ingested enough of the poison to kill an adult. And if by some small chance he did live, he would probably be blind.

And so began our ministry of intercessory prayer.

Confession time. I hate to admit it, but among my immediate thoughts was this sorry one: *I'm going to give this request to our intercessors and they're going to pray for this child's recovery, really believing he's going to be all right, and he'll die (that's what the doctor said and he ought to know), and then they'll be discouraged.*

For fourteen straight weeks I had preached to these people about the incredible power of intercession and they had believed every word of it. They were hyped-up, raring to go, chomping at the bit, ready to charge hell with nothing but a prayer. I had hoped we could start out with something easy and work our way up to the hard stuff. I just knew this was going to be a big let-down.

The request was given to the intercessors, and they came and they prayed. For twenty-four hours these rookies entered the chapel to exercise their priesthood, to besiege the throne of God, to lay down their lives for a brother.

Twenty-four hours after the first phone call, the phone shattered the hush of the chapel once more. It was the mother calling again from the hospital. She was crying, laughing, praising God. The doctor didn't understand it, but her baby was going to recover, and there was no damage to his eyes or any vital organs. Wasn't it wonderful! It had to be a miracle!

And so it was. I had thought it best to launch our intercessory ministry with the possible and work up to the impossible. But God started with the impossible and demonstrated from the very beginning the awesome power of prayer.

Prayer is the secret of Jesus. He has passed it on to us, but not all Christians receive it. The secret of greater works is received only by those who say, "I believe God will do His greatest works through my prayers."

That is the Jesus Secret — for people just like us.

"For Official Use Only"

A man came to my office one day to talk about a serious business problem. After he explained his situation, I asked, "Have you prayed about it?"

He looked offended. "Of course not."

"Why not?"

"Oh, that's business," he said. "I couldn't pray about that."

To my visitor, prayer was "For Official Use Only," official meaning "religious." Yet in prayer everything is considered official business. To the question: For what may I pray? Jesus answers, "Whatever." Not only does Jesus say "whatever" in our model verse, John 14:13, but He also expresses the same thought in John 15:7: "If you abide in Me, and My words abide in you, you will ask what you desire, and it shall be done for you." The Bible encourages us to pray about everything.

Don't Fence Me In

When speaking of prayer, the Bible uses "big" words, limitless words. For example, Jeremiah 33:3: "Call to Me, and I will answer you, and show you great and mighty things, which you do not know." The phrase "mighty things" literally means "things that are hidden, inaccessible, things that are fenced in."

I remember a cowboy song, popular when I was a boy, called "Don't Fence Me In." That's what prayer says: "Don't fence me in." Prayer knocks down the fences and makes things accessible that are otherwise fenced in and off limits. Nothing lies beyond the reach of prayer; there are no boundaries to its jurisdiction.

Prayer is always relevant. Whatever is a concern in the heart of man is a concern in the heart of God. Remember: If it's big enough to worry about, it's big enough to pray about.

Worry about nothing, says Paul, and pray about everything (Philippians 4:6). "Nothing—everything." Prayer touches both ends of our lives and covers everything between.

As we've seen already, Jesus revealed that the church would do greater works than He had done:

> Most assuredly, I say to you, he who believes in
> Me, the works that I do he will do also; and
> greater works than these he will do, because I
> go to My Father (John 14:12).

These greater works, He said, would be done through prayer.

So astonishing were these words that Jesus repeated them—as though He saw incredulity flash across their faces. "Yes, I repeat it, anything you ask for as bearers of My name I will do it for you" (John 14:14, WILLIAMS).

As a matter of fact, during this last meeting with His disciples before His death (John 14-17), Jesus repeated these words six times: "If you ask . . . I will do." Dr. Curtis Mitchell writes:

> In this simple statement, prayer is set forth as the *primary human factor in the accomplishment of God's program on earth.* With a startling boldness, Christ asserted that divine action, in some mysterious manner, is conditioned upon believing prayer. Thus prayer is set forth as the chief task of the believer. It is his responsibility to ask. It is God's responsibility to accomplish.[1]

If I had to pick one verse in the Bible that most adequately and concisely defines prayer, it would be John 14:13: "And whatever you ask in My name, that will I do, that the Father may be glorified in the Son."

In chapter 2 we saw Christ's promise of greater works. Now we see the kind of praying by which these greater works are done.

In My Name

The most significant phrase in that statement is "whatever you ask in My name." In these upper-room chapters (John 14—16) Jesus uses these words several times:

Whatever you ask in My name (14:13).

If you ask anything in My name (14:14).

Whatever you ask of the Father in My name
(15:16).

Whatever you ask the Father in My name, He
will give you (16:23).

Until now you have asked nothing in My name.
Ask, and you will receive (16:24).

In that day you will ask in My name (16:26).

With these words, *in My name,* Jesus signals a
new stage in His redemptive work and a new dimension
in His relationship with His disciples. He had promised
them they would do greater works "because I go to My
Father." Until He ascended to His Father, His redemptive work was incomplete; only when He had sat down
at the right hand of the majesty on high would the
promise be realized. Having by Himself made puri-
fication for our sins, He is become Mediator, the ex-
ecutor of His own testament. He has taken up the reins
of authority (Hebrews 1:3).

"He sat down" — a work completed and a work
commenced. The work of the cross, His shame, suffering and sacrifice finished. The work of the throne,
intercession and mediation begun. It is through Jesus
that men now come to God. No longer in the name of
sacrifices, but in the name of the Sacrifice. No longer
through the mediation of earthly priests, but now
through our Great High Priest who has entered into
heaven, there to appear in the presence of God for us.

To make up for His physical absence, Jesus
promised the disciples three things: His *peace* (John
14:27); the *Paraclete*, or Helper (John 14:16), and *prayer
in His name* (John 16:23,24). Praying in the name of
Jesus is a totally new teaching on prayer and is found
only in the Gospel of John.

What's In a Name?

What is so special about this praying in the name of Jesus? And not only praying in His name, but also *living* in His name? Paul instructs that whatever we do "in word or in deed, do all in the name of the Lord Jesus, giving thanks to God the Father through Him" (Colossians 3:17).

The name of Jesus is not a secret code that works some kind of magical spell when it is invoked, like "Open Sesame!" or "Shazam!" It isn't a tool with which to manipulate God. To pray in the name of Jesus means to pray "by the authority of," "in harmony with," or "sanctioned by" Jesus Christ. He has given us the right to pray in His name because we are His representatives, and we ask as His representatives because we are about His business.

In Luke 9:48 Jesus said, "Whoever receives this little child in My name receives Me; and whoever receives Me receives Him who sent Me." To receive someone in Jesus' name is like receiving Jesus Himself. Jesus is totally identified with His name, and to recognize that name means to recognize fully who He is and what He has done.

Let's look, for example, at Romans 10:13: "Whoever calls upon the name of the Lord shall be saved." This is a part of the "Roman Road to Salvation." I've used it many times in witnessing to lost people. But the verse says more than "if you call on Christ to save you, He will." This statement is not restricted to prayer. The verb *call* used here is first, acclamation, and then invocation.[2]

To "call on the name of the Lord" is to acknowledge that Jesus is what His name says He is: Lord.

Verse 9 says: "If you confess with your mouth the Lord Jesus [cf. verse 13] and believe in your heart that God has raised Him from the dead, you will be saved." His name is Lord, and He is what His name says He is: Lord. And all who acknowledge Him as Lord by calling on His name will be saved.

Now let's gather it all together. To pray or to act in the name of Jesus means that we do so by His authority and with His approval. It also means that what we pray for or what we do is consistent with His character as expressed in His name. You can't lie or steal in Jesus' name; that is inconsistent with His name and He would never grant you authority to use His name in that setting.

To pray in the name of Jesus, then, is to pray according to His will, with His approval, and consistent with His nature, character and purpose. Therefore, it is as though Jesus Himself were making the request. That is our authority.

Blood, Not Sweat

Let me illustrate this with two incidents. When I was pastor of a young, fast-growing suburban church I found that the best hour for my personal prayer time was around midnight—everybody else was asleep and neither the phone nor the doorbell was likely to ring. One particular day had been unusually hectic. It had been consumed by busywork. I hadn't taken time to pray or read my Bible; I hadn't done anything "spiritual." I had written some necessary letters, returned a number of phone calls, planned meetings and worked on the church calendar—but nothing spiritual.

At midnight I came to my prayer time feeling unworthy. The first words out of my mouth were, "Lord, I know I have no right to ask You for anything tonight," and I proceeded to apologize for being too busy to pray, read the Bible, or witness—too busy to do anything spiritual. I was praying like a wimp.

Suddenly it seemed as if the Lord said, "Suppose you had done a lot of 'spiritual' things today—suppose you had prayed for four hours, read the Bible (on your knees) for four hours, and led ten people to Christ. Would you feel more confident praying than you do now?"

"Yes, I would!"

"Then you are praying in your own name! You think I hear you because of your holiness. You think I am more inclined to listen to you if you have done a lot of good works. You are approaching Me in your own unworthy name. If you had prayed for eight hours today and read the Bible on your knees for eight hours, and had led fifty people to Christ, you would have no more right to pray then than you do now!"

I looked down at the floor of the throne room and saw that it was sprinkled, not with the sweat of my good works, but with the blood of His sacrifice.

When Peter and John healed the crippled man at the Beautiful Gate of the temple, Peter said to him, "In the name of Jesus Christ of Nazareth, rise up and walk" (Acts 3:6).

The crowd of people who constantly thronged the temple area were "filled with wonder and amazement at what had happened to him" (verse 10), and they ran toward Peter and John. And . . .

When Peter saw it, he responded to the
people: "Men of Israel, why do you marvel at
this . . . as though by our own power or godliness we had made this man walk?" (Acts 3:12)

The power to heal was not a prize awarded to
them because they were godly. "His name, through
faith in His name, has made this man strong" (Acts
3:16).

God does not welcome us to the throne of grace
because of what we have done, but because of what
Christ has done. We come in Jesus' name, and the
Father receives us in Jesus' name.

Here's a little experiment that may nail this
truth down for you. The next time you pray, tell God
you are coming to Him in your own name, and that you
demand to be heard because of your own righteousness.
I tried it that night. I never felt such utter desolation.
I retreated to the name of Jesus.

More Light

God sent me some more light in a surprising
way. We were in Arkansas visiting my brother and his
family, and the county fair was in full swing. One night
we loaded everybody into the car and went to the fair.
We weren't there long until it became obvious our
children were not interested in the blue-ribbon hogs or
the award-winning heifers. They wanted to get to the
rides. So, abandoning the more cultural aspects of the
fair, we headed for the carnival and cotton candy.

All the rides were ten cents apiece. We bought a
big roll of red ten-cent tickets and got organized. At the
time my brother had one child, Rebecca; I had three—
Ron, Jr., Stephen and Kimberly. I positioned myself at

the entrance of the rides and as the kids came by, holding out their hands, I tore off a red ten-cent ticket and gave it to them.

I was standing at the entrance to the Tilt-A-Whirl with the roll of tickets. First, Rebecca came by, holding out her hand, and I gave her a ticket. Then Kimberly came by with her hand out and I gave her a ticket. Ronnie was next, then Stephen, each holding out his hand for a red ten-cent ticket.

Right behind Stephen came a little boy I'd never seen in my life — holding out his hand for a red ten-cent ticket. *Who is this kid? What's he trying to pull? These tickets cost ten cents apiece — you don't go around giving them away to every kid who has his hand out.* The boy stood there, hand outstretched, waiting. I ignored him. He stood there; the line behind him began to pile up. Would-be Tilt-a-Whirl riders grew restless and demanded to know what the holdup was. Finally, Stephen turned around, pointed to this importunate little beggar and said, "Dad, this is my friend. I told him you would give him a ticket."

Friend! We hadn't been there twenty minutes. I looked down. The boy was still standing there, holding out his hand.

Do you know what I did? I tore off a red ten-cent ticket and gave it to him — not because I wanted to, or because he deserved it, but because my son had told this boy that his dad would give him a ticket. I wasn't about to embarrass my son or make him out to be a liar.

Though he didn't realize it, the little boy was asking for a ticket "in Stephen's name." And I gave him a ticket "in Stephen's name." I made good the word of my son.

Then I saw it. That's it! I go to the Father and say, "Your Son said that if I ask for a red ten-cent ticket, You will give me one." I ask in Jesus' name and the Father gives in Jesus' name.

The Father makes good the word of His Son.

Why God Answers Prayer

At this point we could raise some knotty questions — questions like: Does God change His mind? Does prayer change God's plans? Is God's will a decree or a desire? Or both? Or neither? I'm disinclined to chase after answers to questions like that lest we bog down in speculation and never get around to praying.

Whatever our answers to these or any other questions, they must (1) leave God's sovereignty intact, and (2) leave us where we still have to trust Him. God speaks to us in a language we can understand, and God's Word to us is, *He responds to our prayers*. That's the way He said it and that's the way He intended us to take it.

If we wait until we understand everything about prayer, we'll never pray. Vance Havner used to say, "I don't understand all about electricity, but I'm not going to sit around in the dark till I do." We don't have to understand prayer in order to pray.

How Important Is Prayer?

The important thing is to pray. How important? Only this: There are some things God will do if we ask Him that He will not do if we do not ask Him. We carelessly say, "Well, whatever happens is God's will. If God wants me to have this, I will get it. If it was meant to be, it will be." That is only partially true. The words of Jesus, "If you ask, I will do," carry the obvious implication that if we do not ask, Jesus will not act. James says it plainly enough: "You do not have because you do not ask" (James 4:2).

A Surprising Discovery

For example, I discovered a surprising fact about the healing miracles recorded in the Gospels. Jesus rarely took the initiative in those miracles. Ordinarily, Jesus did not heal people until they asked Him to. Sometimes they almost had to chase Him down. Bartimaeus cried so long and so loud before Jesus stopped to listen that the crowd told that blind beggar to shut up (Mark 10:46-52). Jesus ignored, then "insulted" the Syrophoenician woman before healing her daughter (Matthew 15:21-28). Jairus took the initiative and came to Jesus on behalf of his daughter. The woman with the issue of blood touched Jesus for healing before He ever noticed her.

Look again at our model verse:

And whatever you ask in My name, *that will I do,* that the Father may be glorified in the Son (John 14:13).

In the following verse Jesus repeats the promise: "If you ask anything in My name, *I will do it*" (verse
14, emphasis added). Notice He doesn't say, "I will *help
you* do it." He says, "*I* will do it."

Just for a minute, go back to verse 12 where
Jesus says that "he who believes . . . the works that I
do he will do also . . . and greater works than these he
will do." In one verse Jesus says that *we* will do great
works; then in the next verse He says, "*I* will do it."
Well, which is it — Christ or us?

Both. Both Jesus and we do the works. Remember our discussion of John 14, verses 8 through 10, in
the last chapter? When Philip asked Jesus to show them
the Father, Jesus said that if they had seen Him, they
had seen the Father. The Father acted through His Son.

What was true of the Father and the Son is true
of us also. We do greater works, but it is actually Jesus
doing them through us — in response to our believing
prayer. We often say, "Earth waits for heaven to move."
But we also can say, "Heaven waits for earth to ask."

Why does God do it this way? The most difficult
thing to understand about prayer is why God would
place this kind of power in the hands of people like us.
Why does God delight in answering prayer? Why does
Jesus commit Himself to act when we ask? He tells us
plainly: "that the Father may be glorified in the Son"
(verse 13).

The Supreme Motive

That the Father may be glorified. Here is the
supreme motive of all praying. The big deal about
prayer is not that we get what we ask for, but that God

is glorified in our getting it. This is the plumbline we will return to again and again in this book.

Praying in the name of Jesus is the second of what I call the Big Three that we have met so far. By the Big Three I mean the three qualifiers of all prayer. Every petition is formed within the context of these provisions: (1) the Will of God; (2) the Name of Jesus; and (3) the Glory of God. Nothing done in the name of Jesus would be contrary to God's will or inconsistent with His glory. So it is correct to say that I can pray in the name of Jesus only when what I ask for is according to His will, and when the answer will bring glory to God.

When my motive for asking is the same as His for answering, I'm on praying ground. When I want what He wants, when we both want the same thing, we're in business.

I think God delights in prayer because when He does something by answering, there is no doubt who has done it. Christians, especially we ministers, have a knack for giving God the glory while we take the credit ourselves. In describing some great accomplishment, we share in glorious detail how diligently we planned and studied and surveyed and planned even more, how hard and long we labored to bring this wonderful thing about. Then we are careful to add this postscript: "To God be the glory." It's as though we were tipping a waiter. God gets honorable mention.

On the other hand, when God works in obvious answer to prayer, He gets both the credit and the glory.

WhatAChurch! WhatAPancake!

In my last pastorate our youth choir was invited one summer to participate in a city-wide evangelistic crusade in Salt Lake City. They would perform in shopping malls and parks during the day and in the crusade services at night. Everybody was excited. But we had four thousand problems, and every one of them had a picture of George Washington on it. The trip would cost $4,000 which we didn't have.

Someone suggested we raise the money, and in some moment of sublime unconsciousness I agreed to let the young people stage a pancake breakfast. I've always hated things like that — you know, buy a pancake and lend a hand to a God who has fallen on hard times — that kind of stuff.

I understand the necessity of raising support funds for missionaries and other Christian workers — my wife and I have been helping support several such people for years. But this was something far different.

At any rate, we chose a Saturday and printed a hundred tickets and sold pancakes. I will never forget that fateful Saturday morning, the morning I suddenly recovered from my fit of unconsciousness, and then the sight that greeted my eyes. Our church was next to a hamburger shack called "WhatABurger"; they made huge hamburgers and when you saw one you were supposed to say, "What a burger!" Our church marquee cried, "WhatAChurch! WhatAPancake!" The young people were standing in the middle of the busy street. On their heads they wore chef hats WhatABurger had given them, and around their necks hung placards hawking pancakes. They were enthusiastically flagging down cars, imploring the drivers to stop for a pancake.

I parked my car and, with my head down, looking neither to the right nor to the left, I stepped quickly into the church. There, standing in the foyer, wearing their own silly-looking chef hats from WhatABurger, were my deacons, men "full of faith and the Holy Ghost," cooking pancakes. Tables were set up where a few people, people who did not especially want pancakes but were willing to help God through this crisis, were silently nibbling at what appeared to be some species of pancakes. I stood there as the aroma of Aunt Jemimah pancakes and Log Cabin maple syrup filled the sanctuary of the Lord.

We raised $2,000 that day. For the next three days God banged me over the head with it until I repented of that foolishness. Wednesday afternoon in my study as I prayed about the situation, the Lord seemed to say, "Let Me show you what I can do. Trust Me for the next $2,000 — the whole $2,000 to come through one person."

That night I told the church we still needed $2,000 but we were never again going to do anything like selling pancakes to raise money — at least not while I was pastor. "If God wants this choir to go to Salt Lake City," I said, "He will provide the money in a way that will honor Him and not humiliate His church."

Someone wanted to know what we would do if God did not come through and we didn't get the money.

"We won't go," I said. "Maybe that will be God's way of telling us He doesn't want our choir out there. I believe it was William Carey who said, 'God's work, done in God's way, will never lack God's supply.' "

I shared with them what I felt God had led me to trust Him for that afternoon. The people agreed and we committed it to God, praying that He would supply the need according to His riches in glory.

Then I began to wonder who would give the money. There were two or three people in the church who could do it, but none of them came forward. A few days later, around six in the evening, my phone rang. It was a young woman in our church who had recently married. I knew that both she and her husband had to work to make ends meet.

She said, "Pastor, a few months ago, before I was married, I was in an automobile accident and I received $3,000 from the insurance company. I still have $2,000. All day at work I felt like I should give that for the choir trip, but I didn't want to do anything without talking to my husband. He just came in from work and before I had a chance to say anything to him, he said he felt like God wanted us to give that $2,000 to the youth choir. So that's what we want to do."

We raised $2,000 selling pancakes and $2,000 praying. When we sold the pancakes we thanked the choir members for standing in the middle of the street. We thanked the deacons for giving up their Saturday to cook pancakes; we thanked WhatABurger for the silly-looking chef hats; we thanked Aunt Jemimah for selling us mix at a discount, and Log Cabin as well — and then worried that we might have forgotten to thank someone.

When we raised $2,000 by prayer, we simply thanked the Lord. He got all the glory and all the credit. After all, that's what prayer is all about.

PART TWO

The Secret Kingdom's Secret Weapon

The War
of the Worlds

For we do not wrestle against flesh and blood,
but against principalities, against powers,
against the rulers of the darkness of this age,
against spiritual hosts of wickedness in the
heavenly places (Ephesians 6:12).

An ancient story tells of a wrestler from
Ephesus who was said to be undefeated and un-
defeatable. In match after match he amazed spectators
and overpowered opponents. When he competed in the
Olympia he appeared to be unbeatable as he repeatedly
defeated his adversaries—until the officials discovered
he was wearing the Ephesia Grammata around his
ankle. The Ephesia Grammata (Ephesian letters) were
written magic spells, usually sewn in a bag and worn as
an amulet. They were known to exist as early as the
fourth century B.C. and were supposed to ward off

demons and evil spirits and give the bearer special powers and protection. The officials of the Olympia removed the "letters" from the wrestler's leg, robbing him of his magical powers, and he was easily beaten in three successive events.[1]

Perhaps Paul was thinking of this story when he mixed his metaphors and, in a passage full of military symbols, used an athletic one when he wrote, "We do not wrestle against flesh and blood."

The Ephesians were certainly familiar with both wrestling and magic. Wrestling was extremely popular in the games of western Asia Minor, and Ephesus had a reputation as a magical center. The hellenistic world was obsessed with demons and supernatural powers. Ephesus, the third largest city of the Empire, "was by far the most hospitable to magicians, sorcerers, and charlatans of all sort."[2] The city swarmed with soothsayers and purveyors of charm.

It is interesting to think that Paul might have been saying to his readers that they should no longer "put on" the Ephesia Grammata as a source of power but should "put on" the whole armor of God. In contrast to the flesh-and-blood wrestling they were familiar with, the real struggle of believers "is a spiritual power encounter which requires spiritual weaponry."[3]

Our battle against the powers of darkness is not as simple as the struggle of the wrestler who can easily come to grips with his opponents.

Whatever was in Paul's thoughts, one thing is clear: He meant to awaken his readers to the supernatural warfare they were engaged in.

A Conflict of Powers: The Power of God vs. the Powers of Darkness

The Christian life is a life of conflict. We are at war. Six times in the "warfare passage" of Ephesians 6:10-18, Paul uses the word *against,* a word referring to hand-to-hand combat emphasizing both the intensity of the battle and the personal nature of the fight. It is not a spectator sport viewed from a safe distance. We are in the thick of it, personally involved in the conflict, whether we know it or not.

The Christian is *against* something and something is *against* the Christian. As believers we are the objects of organized assaults by unseen forces, a hierarchy of invisible powers in rebellion against God. Paul identifies these sinister opponents as "principalities," "powers," "rulers," and "spiritual wickedness."

Paul is not describing four different classes of demons. Each term simply views the forces arrayed against God and His people in a different manner. "Principalities" refer to their rank and rule. "Powers" suggest their investment with authority. "World rulers of this darkness" points up their control over a world in revolt against its creator. "Spiritual wickedness in high places" depicts them as an army of wicked spirits inhabiting, or at least bringing their combat to, the heavenly sphere."[4]

Walter Wink writes, "This is a series, a heaping up of terms to describe the effable, invisible, world-enveloping reach of a spiritual network of powers inimical to life."[5] These are not mere metaphors or figures of speech. This battle is real.

The Primary Target

In a sense the primary target in intercession is not the person or the problem; rather, it is the power behind it. And there *are* powers behind these things, deep and dark powers. We must break the habit of taking the visible part for the whole, of confusing what the eye beholds with the ultimate reality. "The consequence of such confusion is . . . slavery to the unseen power behind the visible elements."[6]

We are engaged in spiritual warfare and we must meet the devil on his own ground. In Paul's second letter to the Corinthians, he says we do not fight this war with weapons of flesh, but with the mighty weapons of God (10:3,4). Our warfare is not physical or material, and our weapons cannot be physical or material.

I remember Al. He was the kind of guy you couldn't help but like, no matter how hard you tried not to. Personality plus. Hot shot salesman. Professing Christian. Alcoholic. And when he was drunk, he was abusive to his wife and children.

Al and I talked and prayed dozens of times, sometimes in his home, sometimes in my office. He knew the Bible as well as I did. In our counseling sessions I would start to quote a verse of Scripture and he would finish it, giving chapter and verse. It was unsettling; I couldn't tell him a thing he didn't already know. He wept and prayed and repented, but nothing changed.

Late one night his distraught wife called. Drunk again, Al had become abusive, worse than ever this time. She had taken the kids and fled the house.

As I drove to Al's house, the Lord helped me realize that Al's problem was not the problem — it was the *power* behind the problem. Satan had built a stronghold in Al's life and that stronghold had to be destroyed before Al would ever be free of his drinking.

That night Al and I prayed in the light of 2 Corinthians 10:3,4. In prayer we confronted the satanic stronghold in his life, for the first time exposing it for what it really was, acknowledging and claiming Christ's power over it.

I don't know exactly what happened that night or how it happened, but I *do* know that from that moment until now (more than ten years later) Al never took another drink of alcohol. And his whole life changed.

The church has always been slow to understand the tactics needed for spiritual warfare. We wade into battle armed with beautiful sanctuaries and choreographed programs and high-powered publicity. These things are good, but alone they are useless in spiritual warfare.

Jesus had a way of getting past the surface problem to the power behind the problem. Peter, after making his great declaration concerning the identity of Jesus, proceeded to rebuke the Lord for His talk of going to Jerusalem to die. How did Jesus respond? Did He appeal to Peter's understanding of the Scriptures or present a logical argument for going to Jerusalem? No, He went beyond the problem to the power behind it and said, "Get behind me, Satan!" (Matthew 16:23).

Jesus knew that His conflict was not with the flesh and blood of Simon Peter, but with the spiritual powers of darkness.

When Paul and Silas were in Philippi, a young fortuneteller followed them for many days, saying, "These men are the servants of the Most High God, who proclaim to us the way of salvation" (Acts 16:17,18). How did the apostle deal with this problem? Did he inform the girl of the dangers of occultism and challenge her to change her misguided ways? To the contrary, the Bible says he turned to her "and said *to the spirit,* 'I command you in the name of Jesus Christ to come out of her'" (verse 18, emphasis added). Paul went beyond the problem to the power behind the problem. His warfare was spiritual and he used spiritual weapons.

In any war, to underestimate the enemy is a deadly mistake, and no less so in the spiritual conflict. It is not enough to replace crooked politicians with honest ones, to dismantle corrupt institutions and to repeal unjust laws, to erase pornography and do away with abortion. Writing of the attempt by pro-lifers to win by legislation in state legislatures in the wake of the "Webster" decision, Charles Colson said,

> Even if we were to win in the battleground
> states, that will not be the end of the pro-life
> struggle. True, we will have brought human law
> into conformity to God's law—a good end, but not
> enough. While the law is a moral teacher, law
> alone cannot change people's moral choices.
> Women will still seek out illegal abortions . . . so
> we must work on a more fundamental level than
> legislation alone.[7]

We may win surface battles on these fronts but if the demonic powers behind these evils are not dealt with, then like Hydra, another head will sprout in the place of every one we cut off. Even if we, like Heracles, cut off eight of its nine heads, we will still find the ninth head to be "immortal" and out of the range of our weapons. "Change is possible, but only if the spirit as well as the forms of power are touched. And that spirit can only be spiritually discerned and spiritually encountered."[8]

How do you storm the invisible citadels and attack unseen powers? This is where intercession enters the picture. It is not enough to protest; we must also pray. The ninth chapter of Mark relates the story of a demon-possessed boy and his father. While Jesus was on the mountain with Peter, James and John, the remaining disciples attempted unsuccessfully to cast the demon out of the boy. After Jesus arrived on the scene and delivered the boy,

> His disciples asked Him privately, "Why could we not cast him out?" And He said to them, "This kind can come out by nothing but prayer and fasting" (Mark 9:28,29).

(See chapter 14 for more information on fasting.)

Where's the War?

As we've already seen, Ephesians 6 sheds a lot of light on this question. If we are to wage this spiritual battle successfully we must have spiritual armor and spiritual weapons. Paul tells us what we need in verses 13-17:

> Therefore take up the whole armor of God, that you may be able to withstand in the evil day, and having done all, to stand. Stand therefore, having girded your waist with truth, having put on the breastplate of righteousness, and having shod your feet with the preparation of the gospel of peace; above all, taking the shield

of faith . . . the helmet of salvation, and the
sword of the Spirit, which is the word of God.

Now let's follow Paul closely. First, he tells us
that there really is a war, a spiritual war, requiring
spiritual equipment. Then he tells us to suit up for the
fight — put on the whole armor of God, arm ourselves
with the sword of the Spirit. All right, here I am, Paul;
I'm dressed and ready to go. I have on the helmet of
salvation; I'm holding this big bodyshield of faith; the
belt of truth is buckled tightly to support me and hold
the other pieces of armor in place. My feet are shod with
the readiness to obey God; I've got the sword. Now
where's the war? I'm ready to fight; point me in the
direction of the battle.

And he does: "Praying always with all prayer
and supplication" (verse 18). Is he serious? I've made
intense preparation, I'm wearing an iron suit that
weighs a ton and am wielding this giant sword, and
what does Paul tell me to do? *Pray.*

Go back to verse 14. It begins with the command,
"stand," which is the key word in the whole passage.
After the command to "stand," the rest of verse 14 and
all of verses 15 through 17 are parenthetical. We come
back to the main track at verse 18: "Praying always with
all prayer and supplication." Drop everything between
the "therefore" of verse 14 and the "praying" of verse
18, and you have: "Stand, therefore, praying with all
prayer and supplication." *Prayer is the warfare. It is the
battlefield upon which the spiritual war is waged.* The
battle is won or lost here.

Before we ever step onto the battlefield of
preaching or teaching or witnessing, the outcome has
already been determined on the battlefield of prayer.

This is vividly portrayed in Exodus 17:8-13. The Israelites meet Amalek in the Valley of Rephidim; he blocks the path of Israel and says, "This is as far as you go. If you go any farther it will be over my dead body."

Moses says to Joshua, "Get your men and go down into the valley and fight Amalek, and I'll get on top of the mountain and hold up the rod of God."

I think if I had been Joshua, I might have said, "Moses, I've got a better idea. *You* go down into the valley and *I'll* get up on the mountain."

But Joshua follows Moses' orders and fights Amalek in the valley.

Meanwhile, Moses is on the mountain, with the rod of God, and a strange thing happens. When Moses holds up the rod, Joshua prevails; when he lowers the rod, Amalek prevails. Like a symphonic orchestra, the battle follows the baton of the maestro. After a while Moses tires and his hands become leadweights. On the mountain, the rod of God sinks, and in the valley, Amalek prevails.

Aaron and Hur, with Moses on the mountain, find a stone for Moses to sit on; then, one standing on each side of him, they hold up Moses' hands "until the going down of the sun," and Joshua prevails. I love the understatement of the King James Version: "Joshua *discomfited* Amalek and his people with the edge of the sword" (Exodus 17:13, emphasis added).

Where was the battle decided? In the valley with Joshua? No, it was decided on the mountain with Moses. The victory in the valley is won by the intercession on the mountain. The church could win more battles in the valley if it had more intercessors on the mountain lifting high the rod of God, the name of Jesus.

The battle for lost souls is won by prayer and intercession. Prayer *is* the warfare. Evangelism is not the attempt to win the battle—it is the mopping-up operation. The physical possessions of the church, the buildings, organizations and programs are the trucks we drive onto the field of battle to load up the spoils of the victory won by intercession.

Intercession is the secret weapon of the secret kingdom. The early Christians knew this and, refusing to bow to Caesar, they prayed for him. It is remarkable that both Paul and Peter admonished their readers to pray for and honor the very person who was waging bloody persecution against them—the king (1 Timothy 2:1,2, 1 Peter 2:17).

When Christians knelt in the Colosseum to pray as the lions bore down on them, something sullied the audience's thirst for revenge. Even in death these Christians were not only challenging the ultimacy of the emperor and the "spirit" of the empire but also demonstrating the emperor's powerlessness to impose his will even by death (his will being their acknowledging his ultimacy). The final sanction had been publicly robbed of its power. Even as the lions lapped the blood of the saints, Caesar was stripped of his arms and led captive in Christ's triumphal procession. His authority was shown to be penultimate after all. And even those who wished most to deny such a thing were forced, by the very punishment they chose to inflict, to behold its truth. It was a contest of all the brute force of Rome against a small sect that merely prayed. Who could have predicted that the tiny sect would win?[9]

The Triangle of Prayer

The most frightening sound in the world is a telephone ringing in the middle of the night.

It never happens without reminding me of the psalmist's words:

> He will not be afraid of evil tidings;
> His heart is steadfast, trusting in the LORD
> (Psalm 112:7).

My phone was ringing at 4 A.M. Only a couple of hours earlier I had collapsed into bed after a long trip from New Mexico and I knew this phone call meant another seven or eight hours on the road, with no rest at the end. It was my brother telling me that our mother had died—of cancer, after fifty days in the hospital.

We threw some clothes into a couple of suitcases, dragged the kids out of bed and beat the sun to

71

the highway by an hour. Mercifully, it was a trouble-free trip and we arrived in fair condition.

That was in August. In September, sitting in a friend's house in Colorado, I mentioned Mom's death. My friend suddenly stood up and said, "What day was that?"

I told her the date as she disappeared into another room. In a moment she was back, flipping through the pages of a notebook.

"Here it is," she said. She read the date and the entry. It was a prayer diary, and on that August Sunday morning, long before sunrise, she awoke with a burden to pray for my family and me, an unrelenting burden that stayed with her most of the day.

I couldn't help but think of what Jesus said to Peter in the upper room the night He was betrayed. Having told Peter that Satan was going to sift him as wheat, He said, "But I have prayed for you, that your faith should not fail; and when you have returned to Me, strengthen your brethren" (Luke 22:32).

I'm glad Jesus didn't say, "*If* you return to Me," as though the outcome were uncertain. He said, "*When* you have returned to Me."

A Lesson in Intercession

The intercession of Christ prevented the failure of Peter's faith (his love failed and his courage failed, but not his faith) and opened the way for his recovery.

We are never more like Christ than when we are praying for others. Intercession is laying down our life for our friend; it is bearing one another's burden; it is sharing in the sufferings of Christ. The work of redemption, as I've already said, is the work of intercession. Jesus is interceding, the Holy Spirit is interceding, and we are to intercede. Paul closes his passage on spiritual warfare (Ephesians 6:10-17) with a plea for intercessory prayer:

> Praying always with all prayer and supplication in the Spirit, being watchful to this end with all perseverance and supplication *for all the saints* — and for me, that utterance may be given to me, that I may open my mouth boldly to make known the mystery of the gospel (verses 18,19, emphasis added).

God has made us a royal priesthood with the privilege and the responsibility to pray for one another, which ought to drive us to ask, as did the disciples, "Lord, teach us to pray" (Luke 11:1).

He taught them — and He will teach us.

Jesus answered the disciples' request, first with the "Model Prayer" of Luke 11:2-4, then with the parable of the friend at midnight. The parable is a powerful illustration of intercession, involving three parties. Intercession is a triangle of prayer: one person going to another person to get bread for a third person.

> Which of you shall have a friend, and go to him at midnight and say to him, "Friend, lend me three loaves; for a friend of mine has come to me on his journey, and I have nothing to set before him"; and he will answer from within and say, "Do not trouble me; the door is now shut, and my children are with me in bed; I cannot rise and give to you"? I say to you, though he will not rise and give to him because he is his friend, yet because of his persistence he will rise and give him as many as he needs (Luke 11:5-8).

Intercession Is Bold Praying

Daring, bold, audacious — these are the only adjectives that rightly describe intercessory praying.

The situation in the story called for boldness. The hour was inconvenient — it was midnight. The circumstances were inconvenient — "My children are in bed with me." The Williams version translates it: "My children are packed about me in bed."

It was common in those days for whole families to sleep together, not only for warmth, but also because of a lack of space. The typical one-room dwelling would contain one large mat on which the entire family slept — usually along with a few farm animals. "My children are packed about me in bed." Do you remember those maddening occasions when your baby wouldn't go to sleep? You would sing and hum and rock for an hour. And finally, when the little thing falls asleep, the doorbell rings.

But the barely sleeping baby doesn't dissuade the midnight caller. He bangs on the door and keeps banging until lights come on in the neighbors' houses and dogs start barking.

Daring and boldness — all the intercessors of the Bible had these. We will look at two of those intercessors, Abraham and Moses, in this book. Listen to Abraham as he intercedes for godless Sodom:

> Would You also destroy the righteous with the
> wicked? . . . Far be it from You to do such a
> thing as this . . . Shall not the Judge of all the
> earth do right? (Genesis 18:23-25)

Every time I read that, I have an urge to remind Abraham who he's talking to. That's daring praying.

Moses was another bold intercessor. A drama is unfolding in Exodus 32. While Moses has been with God on the mountain, the people have gone wild. They have forgotten the Lord who saved them and have bowed down to worship a god made with their own hands, a golden calf.

When the people "rose up to play" (verse 6), God rose up to judge:

> And the LORD said to Moses, "Go, get down!
> For your people whom you brought out of the
> land of Egypt have corrupted themselves"
> (verse 7).

His patience is exhausted; He's through with them. Finished. End of story.

> I have seen this people, and indeed it is a stiff-
> necked people! Now, therefore, let Me alone,
> that My wrath may burn hot against them and
> I may consume them (verse 10).

But Moses intercedes for them: "Turn from Your fierce wrath, and relent from this harm to Your people" (verse 12). Notice that God calls them Moses' people, but Moses calls them God's people.

In his prayer, Moses makes two bold statements. **First**, he tells God that destroying His own people will ruin His reputation; the Egyptians will mock and say that God delivered them from Egypt so He could kill them in the mountains (verse 12).

Second, if God does this, He will be breaking His promise and violating His own word: "Remember Abraham, Isaac and Israel, Your servants, to whom You swore by Your own self" that they would inherit the land forever (verse 13).

The result? "So the LORD relented from the harm which He said He would do to His people" (verse 14). Think of it—one man wielding the weapon of intercession saved an entire nation.

Intercession Is Stubborn Praying

The most critical part of the story in Luke 11 is verse 8, where Jesus says:

> I say to you, though he will not rise and give to him because he is his friend, yet because of his persistence he will rise and give him as many as he needs.

The word translated "friend" is a strong one and indicates more than a casual or ordinary acquaintance. It is a term of endearment, "to love as a brother." This is an impossible thing—turning away a man you loved like a brother. No one would do that, no matter the hour. Yet this man does. What we have here are two very stubborn men: one man determined to get bread, the other just as determined not to give it. If this man whose heart is as shut as his door won't give in to brotherly love, what will he give in to? If friendship can't make him open his door, what can?

Importunity. That's the old King James word for persistence. "Because of his *persistence* he will rise and give him as many as he needs." In fact, the word is even stronger than persistence. It is a lack of shame, shamelessness. Most of us would be embarrassed if we created such a commotion and our best friend told us to go away. I would be so humiliated I wouldn't show my face around there for months. Not this fellow. He doesn't even have the capacity to be embarrassed. He was born without a shame nerve; he never feels it.

Therefore, he is persistent — stubbornly, shamelessly persistent. He has gall.

Evidently Jesus considered this shameless stubbornness an advantage in praying because He emphasized it again in the parable of the widow and the unjust judge (Luke 18:1-8). The judge, with no fear of God and no regard for man, refused to aid a widow who came to him seeking justice. This is an unbelievable scenario. How could anyone refuse to help a widow? That's the point.

Although there was no pity in the judge, there was importunity in the widow. The judge said to himself:

> Though I do not fear God nor regard man, yet
> because this widow troubles me I will avenge
> her, lest by her continual coming she weary me
> (verses 4,5).

Yet is emphasized in the Greek text; it is the critical point in this story. It is the widow's "continual coming," not a change of heart on the judge's part, that persuades him.

Incidentally, "weary" (verse 5) is a translation of a word that means to hit someone in the eye, to give that person a black eye. This is a tough widow — the judge was afraid she would beat him black and blue.

Now listen to Jesus' application of the story:

> Then the Lord said, "Hear what the unjust
> judge said. And shall God not avenge His own
> elect who cry out day and night to Him, though
> He bears long with them? I tell you that He
> will" (verses 6-8).

If an unjust judge will surrender to the persistent pleading of a widow, how much more will God honor the persistence of His own people?

Do you recall the Old Testament story about Jacob wrestling with an angel (Genesis 32:24-32)? Something about that has always bothered me. This is an angel that Jacob is fighting, an angel who wants to get away, but Jacob won't let him. "Let Me go, for the day breaks," the angel says.

And Jacob replies, "I will not let You go unless You bless me!" (verse 26)

Now here's what bothers me: Have you ever seen an angel who couldn't break away from a mere human if he really wanted to? Do you believe Jacob was so strong he could pin down an angel? *That fight was fixed.* I believe that while the angel was saying, "Let me go," he was whispering under his breath, "but I hope you don't. Hang on a little longer and you'll get the blessing."

I wonder how many times we have stopped short of the blessing? Would Sodom have been saved if Abraham had not stopped at ten? Could our church, our city, our country see a spiritual awakening if we pray like Jacob: "I will not let you go until you bless me"?

Intercession Is Desperate Praying

Only desperate men and women, propelled by a sense of urgency, truly intercede. Those who are "at ease in Zion" (Amos 6:1) will never man the ramparts of intercession to repel the enemy. The indifferent will not be found among the watchmen set upon the walls who "never hold their peace day or night" (Isaiah 62:6). Battles are not won by the nonchalant. Even if one of these should try to intercede, they will soon be side-tracked into more "practical" endeavors. What praying they might do certainly will be neutralized by their half-heartedness.

A cry of desperation sounds throughout this parable. It would have been easy to convince a casual host to wait for a more practical hour to go banging on his neighbor's door. Unconcern always finds an excuse, deep concern always finds a way. Only desperate people take desperate actions and prevail.

Our Inescapable Responsibility

Vance Havner used to say, "The problem is that the situation is desperate but we're not." We should be! Our inescapable responsibility should make us desperate.

"A friend of mine has come to me on his journey." He has come *to me*. Not to my neighbor, not to my pastor, but to me. He is my responsibility. It was an unwritten law that if a traveler stopped at your door, seeking food and refuge, you supplied his needs. Failure to do so was a serious breach of social obligation and jeopardized the life of the traveler.

There are people who, in their journey, have come to us. They live next door, they sit behind us at school, they work in the same office with us—and we are the only Christians they meet. They are our inescapable responsibility.

A fascinating word is often used in the New Testament when talking of the first Christians. It's the word *scattered,* which is sometimes translated, "dispersed." Luke uses this word in Acts to depict the Christians' reaction to persecution:

> They were all scattered throughout the regions
> of Judea and Samaria . . . Therefore those who
> were scattered went everywhere preaching the
> word (8:1,4).

In Acts 11:19 the word occurs again:

> Now those who were scattered after the perse-
> cution that arose over Stephen traveled as far
> as Phoenicia, Cyprus and Antioch.

Peter uses the same word in 1 Peter 1:1:

> Peter, an apostle of Jesus Christ, To the pil-
> grims of the *Dispersion* [scattering] in Pontus,
> Galatia, Cappadocia, Asia and Bithynia (em-
> phasis added).

The Jewish "diaspora" (dispersion) came about
through deportation and other means, some voluntary,
some not, to have them moved to a foreign land. Peter
uses the word for Jewish believers who are scattered
throughout the world and yet hope to be gathered back
to the land one day.

James uses the word in his epistle:

> James, a servant of God and of the Lord Jesus
> Christ, To the twelve tribes which are scattered
> abroad (James 1:1).

What makes this word so interesting, of course,
is its meaning: "to sow seed throughout, the scattering
abroad of seed by the sower." Because of persecution,
Christians were scattered everywhere. But see what
God was doing—He was sowing seed throughout the
world so there could be a great harvest of souls. The
believers of the twelve tribes of the Dispersion were
sown by God in different fields.

Do you think you just lucked into that particular house on that particular street? Could it be that God wanted a harvest there and you are the seed He planted? Think about it.

You may say your company transferred you to this area and that's the only reason you are here. Perhaps it is more than that. Perhaps God is sowing seed in that community, and your company is the instrument He used to do the sowing, just as He used persecution to plant the early Christians in new lands.

Maybe God planted you where you are because He knew that a friend in his journey would pass your way, and maybe God wants you to identify with his need and in Jesus' name meet that need. This person is your inescapable responsibility.

Our Inadequate Resources

Our inadequate resources should also make us desperate. Listen to the plaintive words of the host, "And I have nothing to set before him" (verse 6). His words echo our own desperation in the face of the life-and-death responsibilities God places within our borders.

"Lord, my neighbor is lost and dying of cancer — and I have nothing to set before Him."

"Lord, I have a teenage daughter facing severe temptation — and I have nothing to set before her."

"Lord, the man I work with . . . his home is breaking up — and I have nothing to set before him."

Who is sufficient for these things? No one — and that should drive us to the throne of grace "that we may obtain mercy and find grace to help in time of need"

(Hebrews 4:16). If the church does not learn to knock boldly at the Father's door, her magnificent sanctuaries will become empty breadboxes, and starving travelers, finding no bread at her doors, will turn away from the choreographed worship, their stomachs still empty and their bellies aching.

If a man gets hungry enough, he'll eat bread from a garbage can. You can be sure that if he walks away from the church empty-handed, the devil will be waiting for him with plenty of garbage-can bread.

I've never forgotten the native evangelist from Khartoum, Sudan, who visited our church one Sunday morning. Before the worship service we knelt in my study and he prayed, "Father, if you don't bless the pastor today, the people will go away hungry." I can still hear the urgency in his voice.

God's Inevitable Reward

Which leads to the final point in our parable: God's inevitable reward. "He will rise and give him as many as he needs" (Luke 11:8). Did he get three loaves? I don't know, but he got as many as he needed. No one goes away from the Father empty-handed. The promise of Christ is:

> If you then, being evil, know how to give good
> gifts to your children, how much more will your
> Father who is in heaven give good things to
> those who ask Him! (Matthew 7:11)

We enter the place of intercession with our *much need* and leave with His *much more*.

There's only one place to get bread—from the Father. There's only one way to get it—by asking.

Gaining
the Position

Throughout my ministry I have been intrigued by the fact that I have seen scores of Christian wives, often the most faithful workers in the church, whose husbands were lost—but I can count on one hand the number of Christian husbands whose wives were lost. A faithful Christian woman with an unsaved husband is routine. A Christian husband with an unsaved wife is rare.

Perhaps that's part of the reason for 1 Peter 3 giving apostolic advice to Christian wives on winning their lost husbands but no similar admonition for Christian husbands with lost wives. Anyway, here is Peter's counsel to wives who want to win their husbands to Christ.

Wives, in the same way be submissive to your
husbands so that, if any of them do not believe

the Word, they may be won over without words
by the behavior of their wives, when they see
the purity and reverence of your lives (1 Peter
3:1,2, NIV).

A wife may win her lost husband to Christ
without saying a word to him about it. Let's face it,
some individuals can be reached by only one person and
in only one way. Here, it is the wife, and it is by her life
that her husband is saved, not by his being dragged to
church, hounded by the pastor, or preached to by the
wife. He sees ("watches attentively" is the meaning) the
purity and reverence of her life.

"Your beauty," Peter continues,

should not come from outward adornment,
such as braided hair and the wearing of gold
jewelry and fine clothes. [Note: Peter is not
saying the wife should not braid her hair, wear
jewelry or fine clothes. There's nothing wrong
with those things, but they will not win the husband to Christ.] Instead, it should be that of
your inner self, the unfading beauty of a gentle
and quiet spirit, which is of great worth in
God's sight (verses 3,4, NIV).

Positional Praying

The wife wins her husband, not by her petition
only, but also by her *position* — the position of submis-
siveness, purity and reverence — and by the unfading
beauty of a gentle and quiet spirit. When she gains this
position, her entire life becomes an act of intercession.
When she cooks his favorite dish and listens to a boring
story about the fish that got away, or endures with
grace the post-season football games, she is interceding.
When, with a Christ-like spirit, she accepts his careless

treatment of her, she is interceding. Every beat of her heart is intercession, every drop of blood that flows through her veins is a petition. Every tear that falls from her eyes because of his indifference is a prayer lifted to God.

This brings us to what I believe is the real key to true intercession. Intercession is more than prayer. Prayer is a form and expression of intercession, but it alone is not intercession. Intercession is not petition. Intercession is *position*. It is not something we do—it is something we are. It is not an exercise we engage in at a certain time of the day—it is a life that we live.

A Good Man Is Hard to Find

In the Ezekiel passage, God sought for a man from among them to make a wall, "to stand in the gap before Him." Here God does not necessarily say He is looking for someone to pray—although that would certainly play a part. He is seeking a man who will assume a certain position and live a certain life.

Jeremiah describes a similar search.

Run to and fro through the streets of
    Jerusalem;
See now and know;
And seek in her open places
If you can find a man,
If there is anyone who executes judgment,
Who seeks the truth,
And I will pardon her (Jeremiah 5:1).

Intercession is gaining a position and then praying from that position. "Positional praying."

In the case of Christ, Isaiah said He "made intercession for the transgressors" (53:12). Isaiah does

not mean that Christ only prayed for transgressors—
He lived for them, and He died for them. His entire life,
His ministry, His humiliation, His agony—all of it was
intercession. The Bible says He is now seated at the
right hand of God—to do what? To make intercession
for us. He assumed a position and is now praying from
that position.

If, then, intercession is a position we live in and
pray from, how is that position gained?

Gaining the Position
STAGE ONE: Identification

Let's look again at the triangle of prayer in Luke
11. The intercessor in our story was called upon to make
several sacrifices. He forfeited his sleep and rest; he
risked his friendship to feed a stranger; the whole affair
was an inconvenience to him. Yet the key sacrifice was
this: He identified himself with the traveler and the
traveler's need.

This man was not hungry, he didn't need bread.
It was the guest who was hungry. Some would think,
*Let him do his own begging then, if he wants it badly
enough.* But this host acted as though he were the
hungry one; he took his guest's place. That is the
essence of intercession.

To intercede, we identify ourselves with the
needs of others. The hurt ones listen for a cry like their
own, a cry that tells them they are not alone. That cry
is our prayer. Their cry cost them plenty and our
affirming cry will cost us . . . something.

We can follow the tracks of Jesus here. When
God set out to redeem mankind He identified Himself
with man by becoming a man and walking where man

walked. God did not come to us as an invisible, inaccessible, unapproachable, unknowable deity. He came to us as a man, with a man's feelings, a man's temptations and a man's limitations. He came so close, John said that "our hands have handled" the very Word of Life (1 John 1:1). The word *handled* is used as of a blind man's groping, emphasizing the realness of the handling.

Jesus' baptism was an act of identification with sinners. The baptism of John was a baptism of confession and repentance. That's why none of the Pharisees lined up to be baptized by John—that would have been an admission of sin. When Jesus asked John to baptize Him, John protested: "I have need to be baptized by You, and are You coming to me?" (Matthew 3:14) There seemed no reason to baptize Jesus—He had no sin.

Yet there was a reason: It was to be clear from the beginning of His ministry that Jesus had come to identify Himself with sinners, and John's baptism (a baptism of repentance) was part of that declaration.

Jesus is named for every need of man: To the hungry He is the Bread of Life; to the thirsty He is the Fountain of Living Waters; to the sick He is the Balm of Gilead; to the dying He is the Resurrection and the Life; to the lonely, the Friend that sticks closer than a brother; to the outcast, the Friend of Sinners. The crescendo of our Lord's identification with man was reached at the cross—there he was "numbered with the transgressors" (Isaiah 53:12).

Again, Moses instructs us. He shows how identification is the prelude to intercession. If we look once more at Moses' prayer in Exodus 32:32, we hear him say to God, "Yet now, if You will forgive their sin—but if not, I pray, blot me out of Your book which You have

written." While there is much we do not understand in
Moses' request, one thing is clear: Moses identified
himself with his people.

Moving to the New Testament, we see that Paul
affords us a glimpse into the mystery of identification
in Romans 9:1-3:

> I tell the truth in Christ, I am not lying, my
> conscience also bearing me witness in the Holy
> Spirit, that I have great sorrow and continual
> grief in my heart. *For I could wish that I myself
> were accursed from Christ for my brethren,* my
> kinsmen according to the flesh (emphasis
> added).

Theologians have spun their wheels in these
verses for years, but again, whatever else Paul may
have meant by these words, one thing is clear: His
burden for his brethren was so great and overwhelm-
ing, he was willing to identify himself with them. That
is intercession. No wonder, then, that in the first verse
of the next chapter we hear Paul declare:

> Brethren, my heart's desire and prayer to God
> for Israel is that they may be saved
> (Romans 10:1).

The preeminent requirement for intercession is
the willingness to identify with the one in need, the
readiness to take his burden. It is, in the purest sense,
laying down our lives for the brethren.

The Law of Spiritual Harvest

Jesus pointed the way to spiritual harvest with:

> Most assuredly, I say to you, unless a grain of
> wheat falls into the ground and dies, it remains

alone; but if it dies, it produces much grain
(John 12:24).

The phrase, "it remains alone," indicts us all.
There is little room for argument here—if our lives do
not bring forth fruit, we have not yet learned to die.

Paul reinforces this in 2 Corinthians. Describing his life, he said that he was . . .

> always carrying about in the body the dying of
> the Lord Jesus, that the life of Jesus also may
> be manifested in our body.
>
> For we who live are always delivered to death
> for Jesus' sake, that the life of Jesus also may
> be manifested in our mortal flesh.
>
> *So then death is working in us, but life in you*
> (2 Corinthians 4:10-12, emphasis added).

Let these words sink in. Here is the law of
spiritual harvest:

> *"Death is working in us, but life in you."*

For Jesus the victory was won in the garden
where He prayed, "Your will be done." When He left
Gethsemane the real issue of the cross was finally and
forever settled. Every intercessor has his own Garden
of Gethsemane where the real battle is waged. In intercession the battle is won or lost at the point of our
willingness to enter into Christ's suffering and identify
ourselves with others to the point of sacrifice.

Gaining the Position
STAGE TWO: Sacrifice

This brings us to the next step toward gaining
the position. The friend at midnight not only *identified*
himself with the need of his guest, acting as if he were

the hungry one, but He also *sacrificed* to meet that need. He gave up physical comfort and convenience to go out into the night seeking bread. Intercession is a ministry of sacrifice.

As the intercessor for transgressors, Christ was the answer to His own prayer. From the cross, He prayed for his executioners: "Father, forgive them for they do not know what they do" (Luke 23:34). Yet the only basis upon which the Father could forgive them was that very act of crucifixion, for without the shedding of blood there is no forgiveness of sin. There can be no true intercession outside the fellowship of Christ's sufferings. Don't ask God to do something unless you are willing for Him to do it through *you*.

Gaining the Position
STAGE THREE: Authority

Then from the host's *identification* and *sacrifice* came *authority* to obtain all he needed from his reluctant friend: "He will rise and give him as many as he needs" (Luke 11:8).

Let's pause here and measure our progress. Here is the pattern of intercession:

Identification with the needs of others.

Sacrifice to meet those needs.

Authority to obtain what is needed.

Moses *identified* himself with his people: "But if not, I pray, blot me out of Your book which You have written" (Exodus 32:32). He *sacrificed* for them, praying and fasting forty days on the mountain. He certainly gained *authority* with God in prayer, for though God did chasten them with plagues, He did not consume His people or cast them away.

Jesus *identified* Himself with man by taking on the form of a servant. He *sacrificed* Himself for man by taking our sins in His own body on the tree. And with all *authority* in heaven and earth, He loosed man from his sins, stripped Satan of his armor, tore the stinger out of death and flung open the gates of glory.

Jesus. Moses. Paul. We follow in their trail. The servant is not above his master. Make no mistake about this: Prevailing intercession will cost us — sleepless nights, unseen tears, the sacrifice of personal desire and convenience, and whatever else is necessary to fill up that which is lacking in the sufferings of Christ (Colossians 1:24). When "Zion travailed, she brought forth her children" (Isaiah 66:8). Nature itself teaches us there can be no life without travail.

Only as death works in us will life work in those for whom we pray. That is the law of spiritual harvest. I believe when we, in order to stand in the gap for another, take to ourselves death to advantage and ambition, to consideration, comfort and convenience, then and only then do we have a right to expect a harvest.

Are we willing to assume that position?

Praying
for Others

One summer I took my family to the south coast of Texas, thinking that the gentle rhythm of the waves sliding back and forth across the Gulf Coast beaches might wash a little calm into our souls.

It had not been a good year and it was only half over. A few days before we left, our youngest son added variety to the situation by breaking his leg.

He now wore a cast from his hip to his toes. The x-rays showed not only the break but some tumor-like growths on the bone. Too soon yet to know what they were. I used my imagination.

So there we were, soaking up the sun and surf at in-season rates. And every morning when I woke up, there *he* was, my gloomy companion: depression. He was waiting for me beside the bed—the waves had not washed him away. I couldn't shake him. We went everywhere together, me and my shadow.

Until Thursday morning. I woke up and he wasn't there. I was suspicious. All day long I expected him to leap out from some dark alley, but there wasn't a sign of him. I relaxed from the inside out. Not a single thing had changed but everything was different.

Back home a few days later, I went to my office to pick up the mail that had piled up while I was away. One of the letters bore an unfamiliar hotel logo but I recognized the handwriting. It was from a friend who knew everything about my situation. Next to the date was the time the letter had been written: 3 A.M.

> *Dear Ron . . .*
>
> *I have prayed for you today and am about to pray again that God will make this time through which you are passing a new door open to the mystery of truth. God must love you so much to watch you pass through this trying time . . .*
>
> *So, no sermons at this point. I am going to say the thing that means the most to me at this moment with reference to you. I have no friend on the face of the earth whose friendship I treasure more than yours. I have asked God to put on my heart as much burden as He can to lighten yours. I want to bear it with you. That does not require conversation or correspondence. But in the spiritual realm where those transactions are made, I have asked God for your burden . . .*

I was not surprised to see that the date on the letter was the Thursday I awoke without my sepulchral companion waiting for me.

Is this what Paul had in mind when he told us to bear one another's burdens? Is this what Martin

Luther meant when, feeling unusually strong and happy, he would say, "I feel as if I were being prayed for"? This is surely what T. DeWitt Talmadge had in mind when he said, "The mightiest thing you can do for a man is to pray for him."

Again, the Triangle of Intercession

Prayer was certainly the mightiest thing the early church did for Peter. Around the time that Paul and Barnabas were on their way to Jerusalem with aid from the church at Antioch, Herod the King began to terrorize the young church (Acts 12:1). First, he killed James, the brother of John. That delighted the Jews so much that he booked Peter for the next execution. He seized the apostle and threw him in jail, assigning sixteen men to guard him. In the morning Peter would follow James down the bloody path to martyrdom. But . . .

> Peter was therefore kept in prison, *but* constant prayer was offered to God for him by the church (Acts 12:5, emphasis added).

Note the contrast: Peter was kept in prison — BUT — the church was constantly praying for him. Peter imprisoned and facing death was not the last word on the matter; the last word was, and still can be, "Prayer was offered to God for him by the church."

Don't you find it interesting that the martyrdom of James merits only eleven words in the New King James Version and only seven words in the Greek text? Hardly front-page coverage for a VIP. Yet Peter's episode requires seventeen verses. The story is told in a deliberate manner to highlight the confrontation taking place. It is the conflict between the world and the church, a conflict that persists to this day. It is political power pitted against spiritual power.

Luke writes the story like a novelist. The details are delicious. Herod delivered Peter to four four-man squads, sixteen guards; Peter was rescued the very night Herod intended to bring him out for execution; he slept between two guards, bound by two chains; guards were at the door which was an iron gate; an angel stood by Peter, kicked him awake, and told him to get up, gird himself, tie on his sandals, put on his garment and "Follow me."

They went past the first guardpost and the second guardpost. Then came the iron gate of the city, "which opened to them of its own accord" (verse 10), literally, "automatically." Luke is enjoying himself. He is reveling in the triumph of the praying church.

Is there a better picture of the triangle of intercession than the praying of this young church? Constant prayer (1) to God, (2) for Peter, (3) by the church.

The first church knew it existed—as did its Founder—in deadly conflict with the world. It also knew that its power to confront and conquer the enemy lay in prayer. What it did not know was how much power it had—but it was about to find out.

Once Peter was safely outside the prison, the angel left him. When Peter came to himself and realized he wasn't dreaming, that he had truly been delivered by the angel of the Lord, he headed straight for Mary's house where he knew his fellow believers would be gathered.

When he knocked at the door, a girl named Rhoda went to answer.

> When she recognized Peter's voice, because of
> her gladness she did not open the gate, but ran
> in and announced that Peter stood before the
> gate (verse 14).

Isn't that tremendous? God had answered their prayers—Peter was standing at the door! While they were knocking at heaven's door with a request, God was knocking at their door with the answer!

And what did the church say to Rhoda when they heard her news? Are you ready for this? They said, *"You're crazy!"*

> They said to her, "You are beside yourself!" Yet
> she kept insisting that it was so. So they said,
> "It is his angel."

> And Peter continued knocking; and when they
> opened the door and saw him, they were
> astonished (verses 15,16).

There's encouragement here for us. We romanticize the first Christians so much we think they were perfect, that their faith was without a hint of doubt. These verses plainly show that was not the case. Like Elijah, they were people with a nature like ours (James 5:17)—but they prayed. And God answered, even though they were slow to believe. Sometimes God answers our prayers, not because of our faith, but because of His grace.

The apostle Paul believed in praying for others. His letters are sprinkled with prayers; he moves easily and naturally from talking to his readers about God to talking to God about his readers. In turn he coveted the prayers of his churches, asking for prayers in every letter he wrote—except the letter to the backslidden Galatians.

What an indictment! To what depths of selfish carnality have we plummeted to make our prayers not worth asking for?

What an honor! To think someone has such confidence in our audience with God that they ask us to call their name to Him.

.What a shame! Someone solicits our prayers and we carelessly say, "Of course," but a promise lightly made is easily forgotten—until we receive a note, thanking us for our prayers.

What a responsibility! Pick a church—any church—and thumb through its membership roll. You may be surprised at the number of people on the roll who are never in church. At one time they were there, but not now, not for a long time.

The Survival Rate of the Newborn

Do you know someone like that? I'm sure you do. Christianity is littered with discarded disciples; membership rolls groan under the weight of Demases who have forsaken the Lord for the love of the world (2 Timothy 4:10). We shake our heads and wonder what happened to them. Perhaps they weren't sincere to begin with. As a matter of fact, now that you mention it, I did have a reservation or two about that one—you know, with his background and all.

But let me ask a question. Did we pray for that infant in the faith? When we first noticed signs of decay, when we began to suspect that the enemy had made a bridgehead in his new life—did we pray? Did we take the burden upon our own heart and bear him to the throne of grace and build a protective wall of prayer around him?

The pain of childbirth is twofold: There is the pain of bringing the child into the world, and there is the pain of bringing the child *up* in the world. And the latter is greater. The physical pain of bearing a child is great but usually lasts only a few hours. The pain of *rearing* that same child lasts a lifetime and never subsides. Lewis Smedes says, "When you conceive a child, you covenant to suffer."[1]

Paul knew the pain of both childbirth and childgrowth. Writing to the Galatians (the ones he *didn't* ask to pray for him), he said:

> O my dear children, I am suffering a mother's birth pang for you *again*, until Christ is formed in you (Galatians 4:19, WILLIAMS, emphasis added).

His parental concern shows itself in all his writings, especially Ephesians, Philippians and Colossians. He cradled his children in the arms of intercession.

A Good Work Begun; A Good Work Completed

I love Paul's words to his Philippian converts:

> Being confident of this very thing, that He who has begun a good work in you will complete it until the day of Jesus Christ (Philippians 1:6).

Would to God every pastor could say that about his church members. But before the word of assurance in verse 6, Paul said something else in verses 3 and 4:

> I thank my God upon every remembrance of you, always in every prayer of mine making request for you all with joy.

The intercession of verse 4 precedes the declaration of verse 6. Could there be a connection? Perhaps if we could say, "I am always praying for you," we could also say, "I am confident that what God has started He will complete."

Paul has something even more compelling to say to these believers. Philippians is a thank-you note from Paul to the church at Philippi, thanking them for their much-welcomed gift (4:10) and assuring them that, although unjustly jailed by the authorities and unfairly treated by some of the brethren, he was doing great. As a matter of fact, rather than worrying about him, they should rejoice because all of this "will turn out for my salvation through your prayer and the supply of the Spirit of Jesus Christ" (verse 19).

These things, designed to harm Paul and hinder his work, will actually turn out for his "spiritual welfare" (the meaning of "salvation" here). Instead of thwarting his work, the circumstances advance it.

Paul's heart had been set on going to Rome. In Acts 19:21 he declared, "I must see Rome." And see Rome he did—but not the way he had planned. He expected to stride into the great city as an ambassador for Christ, unashamedly proclaiming the gospel. Instead he was led into Rome dragging the chains of a prisoner.

Still, he insists, this has made his mission all the more successful—he has testified for his Lord in Caesar's palace, and "it has become evident to the whole palace guard, and to all the rest, that my chains are in Christ" (Philippians 1:13).

The adversities the Philippians were anxious about had actually turned out for the greater progress of the gospel.

Supplications and Supply

Then Paul tells them how this will be accomplished: God will use two instruments — "your prayer" and the "supply of the Spirit of Jesus Christ" (verse 19).

Now stop and think about that. Let it sink in. It is not news that the Spirit of God "helps in our weaknesses" (Romans 8:26). We know about the supply of the Spirit. But what is this about "your prayer"? Paul is saying that the prayers of the Philippians are just as necessary to his deliverance as the supply of the Spirit. And I could point out that he mentions the prayers of the saints *first.* Did you know your prayers were that important?

Commenting on this verse, Karl Barth said,

> The prayer of the Philippians is not too unimportant, not too human, not too impotent to stand next to the first Magnitude (the Holy Spirit), next to whom, strictly speaking, no second can stand.[2]

Paul knew three things: (1) He knew the Philippians were praying for him; (2) he knew that when they received his letter, they would pray even more for him; and, (3) he knew their prayers would bring the blessings of God upon him.

This same thought is found in 2 Corinthians. Paul describes the burdens of his ministry as having "the sentence of death in ourselves" (2 Corinthians 1:9); but his confidence is in the . . .

> God who delivered us from so great a death, and does deliver us; in whom we trust that he will still deliver us . . . *you also helping together in prayer for us* (verses 10,11, emphasis added).

When I was a pastor I carried in my pocket a little black book listing the names of church members I was praying for especially—individual needs, special requests, things like that. Inadvertently, I mentioned my little black book in a sermon one Sunday morning. Afterward I was deluged with people asking two questions: Were their names in my book? And, Would I add the name of a person they were concerned about?

I was amazed at their interest—and frightened by their confidence—in my praying. You want to know the most common request? Wives who wanted their husbands' names placed in the book. And into the book they went. Beside the names of those husbands who were Christians but spiritual drop outs, I wrote a request of my own: "Lord, make them hungry," based on Deuteronomy 8:3:

> So He humbled you, *allowed you to hunger*, and
> fed you with manna which you did not know
> (emphasis added).

My prayer was that God would fill these husbands with a holy dissatisfaction with themselves and a hunger for something more. It's hard to believe, but without exception, God did afflict every one of those husbands with a spiritual hunger they never before had experienced, and we saw real revival—in both the church and the homes involved.

God has chosen to work through His people— and through their prayers. Paul believed the prayers of the saints were as important as the supply of the Spirit.

Now all that remains is for us to believe it, too.

God's Prayer List

Prayer was God's idea.

This is an important piece of information. I say that because in times past — and in times present — I've had some real struggles with prayer. I mean, the idea of prayer raises some tough questions and some seemingly valid objections. I bet you've had similar questions.

Questions like: What about the "free will" of man? How can I ask God to save a person who doesn't want to be saved? How can I pray for a carnal Christian who doesn't want to be cured of his carnality? How do you reconcile prayers like that with the will of man?

And the sovereignty of God — isn't God going to do whatever He wants to, anyway? And then there's predestination, for heaven's sake! I mean, God's elect are God's elect, aren't they? Can my prayers shift someone from the reject column to the elect column?

The solution to this dilemma?

Prayer was God's idea. That means all the questions and objections and contradictions surrounding prayer — well, they're God's problems.

For myself, I only need to keep in mind two facts: (1) God commands me to pray. Whether I understand how prayer works or not, whatever the problems encountered, I am commanded to pray. My failure to understand does not excuse my failure to pray. Whether I understand anything else about prayer or not, I know this much: God assures me that my prayers will make a difference.

(2) Whatever God does, He will be consistent with Himself. He will not deny or contradict Himself. I don't know how He resolves the apparent conflict between my prayers and the free will of man, but if it doesn't bother God, I'm not going to let it bother me.

Not only has God commanded us to pray (actually I prefer "invited" because prayer is as much a privilege as it is a command), but He also has given us a prayer list to guide us in our intercession.

We find God's prayer list in Paul's words to Timothy:

> Therefore I exhort first of all the supplications, prayers, intercessions, and giving of thanks be made for all men. For kings and all who are in authority, that we may lead a quiet and peaceable life in all godliness and reverence (1 Timothy 2:1,2).

Paul is giving his young protegé a course in pastoral ministry, and the first thing you should do when your people come together, he says, is to pray. First on the agenda of worship—first, not in sequence necessarily, but first in importance. "First of all," chief above every other exercise, "pray." Prayer is the supreme exercise of worship. The church can do nothing greater than this.

Pray for Secular Leaders

There are some surprises in this prayer list. First, Paul tells us to pray for *secular leaders:* "for kings and all that are in authority." Kings? Are we to pray for the king? That's the fellow who's slaughtering Christians as fast as the lions can eat them. Pray for him? Right, I'll pray for him—I'll ask God to dump fire and brimstone on his unbelieving head.

That's not what Paul had in mind.

Paul's admonition here underscores his conviction that the secular state is instituted by God for the welfare of man. He emphasizes this in his letter to the Romans (which in itself is a telling point!):

> Let every soul be subject to the governing
> authorities. For there is no authority except
> from God, and the authorities that exist are
> appointed by God (Romans 13:1).

Peter, addressing believers immersed in persecution, says:

> Therefore submit yourselves to every ordinance
> of man for the Lord's sake, whether to the king
> as supreme, or the governors, as those who are
> sent by him for the punishment of evil doers
> and for the praise of those who do good. *For
> this is the will of God,* that by doing good you
> may put to silence the ignorance of foolish men
> (1 Peter 2:13-15, emphasis added).

"All who are in authority" are those in places of prominence and high positions. The phrase embraces everyone in a position of authority over us — employers, schoolteachers, parents, church leaders and government leaders.

A couple of points we should touch on are, **first**, the significance of Paul's use of the plural, "kings." Paul does not refer to the present king or emperor only, but to those who follow also — which makes this of permanent application to the church.

Second, Paul does not have in mind prayer primarily aimed at the kings' conversion to Christ. Kings do not have to be Christian kings to be equitable and honorable rulers. Here Paul is thinking of prayer for them in their role as rulers, as men who carry heavy burdens of responsibility and exert powerful influence on the lives of citizens. God's providence is impartial, His rain falling on the just and the unjust, and so should our prayers be, praying even for those who spitefully use us and persecute us (Matthew 5:44). Even non-Christian rulers need the support of our prayers, for no matter how wicked rulers may be, anarchy is worse.

By praying for them like this, the church helps those in authority to exercise their powers wisely and justly. This is obvious as Paul unfolds the motive for such prayer: "that we might lead a quiet and peaceable life in all godliness and reverence" (1 Timothy 2:2). When rulers rule properly, their subjects can live quiet and peaceable lives, the opposite of which is unrest and disturbance — two words that graphically describe our present world.

Good rulers make good government, which in turn makes life quiet and peaceful, which in turn creates a favorable environment for preaching the gospel, and "this is good and acceptable in the sight of God our Savior, who desires all men to be saved and to come to the knowledge of the truth" (verses 3,4). Praying for others: The word of God commands it; the will of God demands it.

Pray for Spiritual Leaders

Some years ago I heard an evangelist announce his sermon title for the following night: "How to Fire Your Pastor." That was too tantalizing to pass up; the next evening the building was packed. Groans of disappointment from the congregation and sighs of relief from a number of ministers filled the air when the evangelist revealed the secret: "If you want to fire your pastor," he thundered, "pray for him! Pray that the Holy Ghost will fall on him and set him afire!"

Of course, they called him a sensationalist, but he got his point across. If you don't like your minister, change him—pray for him. It is uttered often in ministerial circles that great preachers make great churches. That may be true, but it is also true that great churches make great preachers. Better praying in the pew will make better preaching in the pulpit.

God's Blessings on Their Public Ministry

One of the chief characteristics of Paul's letters is his constant appeal for the prayers of his converts. In Ephesians 6:18, he writes:

> Praying always with all prayer and supplication
> in the Spirit . . . for all the saints—*and for me*
> that utterance may be given to me, that I may
> open my mouth boldly to make known the
> mystery of the gospel (emphasis added).

Again in Colossians 4:3,4:

> Meanwhile praying also for us, that God would
> open to us a door for the word, to speak the
> mystery of Christ . . . that I may make it
> manifest, as I ought to speak.

Christians should pray regularly for their pastors, missionaries and evangelists, that God would throw open doors of opportunity and enable them to preach Christ courageously and clearly.

The Romans' Prayers Answered

Paul made a three-fold prayer request of the believers in Rome:

> Now I beg you, brethren . . . that you strive
> together with me in your prayers to God for
> me, [1] that I may be delivered from those in
> Judea who do not believe, and [2] that my service for Jerusalem may be acceptable to the
> saints, [3] that I may come to you with joy by
> the will of God, and may be refreshed together
> with you (Romans 15:30-32, emphasis added).

One of my New Testament professors, Dr. Huber Drumwright, pointed out how that three-fold prayer was answered.[1]

First, when Paul arrived in Jerusalem with the offering for needy believers, he was set upon by his enemies (Acts 21:27). He was rescued by, would you believe it, Roman soldiers! But Paul's enemies didn't give up. They plotted to assassinate him. A young boy, Paul's nephew, overheard the plotters, and when he told Paul and Paul told the Roman centurion, the centurion employed several hundred soldiers to get Paul out of town (see Acts 23:23).

Second, Paul asked the Roman Christians to pray that his service might be acceptable to the saints in Jerusalem. It may come as a surprise to us, but not everybody liked Paul. He was a controversial figure in the early church. He was often criticized, lied about and misunderstood by fellow Christians. So his request for prayer was a serious one. Luke records the answer to that prayer with these words:

> And when we had come to Jerusalem, the
> brethren received us gladly (Acts 21:17).

Paul's **third** request was that he might "come to you in joy by the will of God and find refreshing rest in your company." Luke tells us that Paul's trip to Rome had its moments of terror. First, they encountered a terrible storm that threatened the lives of all on board the ship, but God gave Paul a word of assurance:

> Do not be afraid, Paul; you must be brought
> before Caesar; and indeed God has granted you
> all those who sail with you (Acts 27:24).

After fourteen days, the ship went aground and broke up, but everyone made it to shore safely.

Then, as Paul was carrying a bundle of sticks for a fire to warm and dry out by, a snake, caught in the sticks, bit Paul's hand. The others expected Paul to die from this attack, which to them was a sure sign Paul was a murderer. But Paul shook off the snake, and to the amazement of everyone, was totally unaffected by the bite.

Paul did get to Rome—and it was the intercessions of the Roman Christians, praying in accord with God's will and purpose, that brought him there.

God's Protection on Their Private Lives

Just a few hours ago I watched on TV the sad spectacle of another high-profile minister stepping down from the pulpit amid charges of immoral conduct. He joins a growing number of fallen ministers. I do not believe these few men are representative of most ministers of the gospel, but I have been in the ministry more than thirty years and, while there have always been instances of moral failure, I've never seen anything like this. I have no doubt that the enemy has mounted a massive offensive to discredit ministers of the gospel. Like a roaring lion, he seeks to devour spiritual leaders, and many already have been caught in his jaws.

Few people are as vulnerable to gossip and innuendo as Christian workers. What the world winks at in others, it mocks in ministers. We all feel the blow. That's why Paul spurred the Thessalonian believers to hedge him and his colleagues with protection:

> Finally brothers, pray for us . . . that we may
> be delivered from unprincipled and wicked
> men; for not all have faith (2 Thessalonians
> 3:1,2, WILLIAMS).

Paul's request here is imperative, and the tense of the verb is continuous. He is not asking to be remembered occasionally, "as the Lord may bring me to mind." He is pleading for continuous, vigilant prayer support.

A word, a suspicion, a raised eyebrow—it takes little more than this to destroy the ministry of a person and the testimony of a church. Intercession can build a wall of protection around our spiritual leaders. Such "prayer produces what Raymond Johnson has called 'an antiseptic atmosphere,' in which blasphemy, self-

ishness, greed, dishonesty, immorality, cruelty and injustice find it hard to flourish."[2]

When I see the President on TV, I am always
impressed with the number of Secret Service agents
surrounding him. As was so vividly demonstrated in the
1981 assassination attempt on President Reagan, it is
the job of the Secret Service agents to protect the life
of their President, even if it means throwing themselves
in the path of the bullet.

That's what our spiritual leaders need, a Secret
Service of intercessors — spiritual bodyguards, if you
will — who protect their charges with the shield of
prayer.

Praying With Paul

Much of our praying should be directed to building up believers. Again, Paul is our example; the prayers in his epistles prove this was a concern in his own
prayer life. They provide a Spirit-inspired answer to the
question: How should I pray for other Christians?

Believers need to realize their unlimited resources in Christ. Listen to Paul pray:

> That the God of our Lord Jesus Christ, the
> Father of glory may give to you the spirit of
> wisdom and revelation in the knowledge of
> Him . . . that you may know what is the hope
> of His calling, what are the riches of the glory
> of His inheritance in the saints . . . the exceed-
> ing greatness of His power toward us who
> believe (Ephesians 1:17-19).

Think what it would mean to a Christian about
to go down for the count before the tempter to suddenly
realize that the power that raised Jesus from the dead

dwells in him, and is available to him at that very moment. These are the people we should pray for.

Ephesians 3:14-19 is a treasury of biblical petitions. Paul bows his knees to the Father and prays for the believers at Ephesus:

- that they would be STRENGTHENED WITH MIGHT through His Spirit in the inner man;

- that CHRIST MAY DWELL IN THEIR HEARTS through faith;

- that they would be ABLE TO COMPREHEND THE LOVE OF CHRIST; and

- that they might be FILLED WITH THE FULL-NESS OF GOD.

Another rich prayer list is found in Philippians 1:9-11. Paul prays specifically for these Christians:

- that their LOVE MAY ABOUND MORE AND MORE;

- that they may APPROVE THINGS THAT ARE EXCELLENT;

- that they may be SINCERE AND WITHOUT OFFENSE;

- that they may be FILLED WITH THE FRUITS OF RIGHTEOUSNESS.

One more example, Colossians 1:9-12. Here Paul prays that the Colossian Christians:

- will be FILLED WITH THE KNOWLEDGE OF GOD'S WILL;

- might walk WORTHY OF THE LORD UNTO ALL PLEASING;

- will be FRUITFUL IN EVERY GOOD WORK;

- will INCREASE IN THE KNOWLEDGE OF GOD;

- will be STRENGTHENED WITH ALL MIGHT; and

- will LIVE A LIFE OF CONTINUAL THANKSGIVING.

Some Suggested Supplications

Now let's scoop up some of these Pauline prayers, mix them together and draw out a list of scriptural supplications. Certain friends may come to mind as you read through the list. These probably are the ones you should pray for first. When you pray for others, pray that

- their eyes will be open to their unlimited resources in Christ;

- they will be strengthened by the Holy Spirit;

- they will be filled with the fullness of God;

- they will fully understand and appreciate the love of Christ;

- their love for others will grow to overflowing;

- they will be able to discern right from wrong and make the right decisions in all matters;

- they will be free of all pretense and hypocrisy and live a blameless life;

- they will be full of the fruits of righteousness;

- they will know God's will for their lives and be committed to it;

- they will please God in everything they do;

- they will be fruitful in every good work;

- they will hunger and thirst to know more and more about God.

I don't mean that this list should be a string of prayer beads to chant over with the names of those you pray for. These are scriptural suggestions, and you just rephrase them according to the needs of those on your prayer list.

Remember, God works through our prayers to bring the supply of the Spirit into the lives of needy believers. By praying for others we can bring the power of Jesus into a person's life. We can apply His healing power to wounded hearts. We can say with Paul that we are "confident of this very thing, that He who has begun a good work in [these] will complete it until the day of Jesus Christ."

In 1650 Jeremy Taylor wrote a book called *The Rules and Exercises of Holy Living*. He said this about prayer:

> Christ hath put it [the power of prayer] into the hands of men, and the prayers of men have saved cities and kingdoms from ruin; prayer hath raised dead men to life, hath stopped the violence of fire, shut the mouths of wild beasts, altered the course of nature, caused rain in Egypt and drought in the sea. Prayer rules over all gods; it arrests the sun in its course and stays the chariot wheels of the moon; it reconciles our suffering and weak faculties with the violence of torment and the violence of persecution; it pleases God and supplies all our need.

Praying for the Lost

Afew years ago I was invited to give a series of lectures on prayer at a well-known evangelical seminary. At their request I sent manuscripts of each of the five messages I would deliver, including one titled, "Praying for the Lost."

Several weeks later I received a letter from a member of the chapel lecture committee asking if I would substitute another message for the one on praying for the lost, which, of course, I did. It was the stated position of the seminary president that praying for the lost to be saved was unscriptural.

I've always regretted that he and I didn't have a chance to discuss the matter, because I believe it was largely a matter of semantics. If we had talked about it, this chapter is what I would have said.

Can We Pray for the Lost?

The prayer of Jesus in John 17 is often pointed to as evidence that we are not to pray for the lost. In His prayer, Jesus said, "I ask on their behalf, I do not ask on behalf of the world, but of those whom Thou hast given Me; for they are Thine" (verse 9, NAS).

This is arguing from inference. At that moment Jesus was praying for His followers only, not for the world. There is no suggestion that the world was never to be prayed for; at that precise moment, in that specific prayer, Jesus did not pray for the world, but He did not say we should never pray for the world. Only a few hours later, Jesus prayed for a part of that lost world when He cried on the cross, "Father, forgive them, for they know not what they do."

The apostle Paul saw no problem in praying for the unsaved Jews: "Brethren, my heart's desire and my prayer to God for them is for their salvation" (Romans 10:1, NAS).

In 1 John 5:14,15, we have this promise:

Now this is the confidence that we have in Him, that if we ask anything according to His will, He hears us; and if we know that He hears us, whatever we ask, we know that we have the petitions that we have asked of him.

Couple that promise with these statements:

The Lord is not slack concerning His promise, as some men count slackness; but is longsuffering toward us, not willing that any should perish but that all should come to repentance (2 Peter 3:9).

[God] desires all men to be saved and to come to the knowledge of the truth (1 Timothy 2:4).

The will of God is clearly stated in these verses. Christ's death on the cross established the fact that God is not willing that any should perish. When we pray for the lost to be saved, we are praying within the revealed will of God. To say that we may not pray for the lost to be saved is to deny ourselves the mightiest power God has given us to accomplish our greatest task.

God has always used intercessors to achieve His will. Intercession has postponed, even prevented, the wrath of God from coming upon an individual or a nation. In Job 42, God told Eliphaz and his two friends to go to Job and let him pray for them, "lest I deal with you according to your folly" (verse 8). We already have seen that the intercession of Moses saved his nation from the judgment of God. When God destroyed Sodom and Gomorrah, He spared Lot because He remembered Abraham's intercession.

The four men who lowered their crippled friend through the ceiling to get him to Jesus were "intercessors." The Bible says:

> When [Jesus] saw their faith, He said unto [the man sick of the palsy], "Man, your sins are forgiven you" (Luke 5:20).

Jesus saw *their* faith. Whether the sick man had faith is not mentioned. It was the faith of his friends that secured the healing.

The simple, yet profound fact is that God responds to prayer. Because we pray, He does things that He would not otherwise do (see chapter 2). That God would place such an incomparable privilege and such responsibility in our hands is past understanding—but He has done just that. Through intercession we can become the instrument of salvation to men and women we never see face to face in this life. We can become, in one moment, a missionary to the farthest corners of the earth. With the arms of intercession we can embrace the world and lift it to God in prayer.

Seeking and Saving

What did Jesus mean when He said, "For the Son of Man has come to seek and to save that which was lost" (Luke 19:10)? It must mean . . .

> more than a mere attempt to locate unsaved men, for they are present on every hand. The term . . . suggests a divine preparation of the unsaved that will bring them into adjustment with the necessary conditions of salvation.[1]

Divine Preparation of the Unsaved

This is seen in the episode of Philip and the Ethiopian eunuch (Acts 8:26-40). The Ethiopian was returning from Jerusalem where he had gone to worship and, sitting in his chariot, he was reading about the Suffering Servant in Isaiah. At that precise moment (Greek: "as he ran, he was reading"), Philip, obeying the Spirit, joined the man and asked if he understood what he was reading. Now that's what I call preparation. Before Philip ever saw the Ethiopian, before the Spirit ever told him to join the man, God had been preparing the man's heart to hear about Jesus. And when the man was ready, God dispatched Philip to complete the task.

The same was true of Cornelius, the centurion (Acts 10:1*ff.*). Only after Cornelius was prepared to hear the gospel did God summon Peter. Cornelius was ready to be saved before Peter was ready to tell him how.

Preparation *for* salvation is part of the work *of* salvation. To the Thessalonians, Paul said:

> We are bound to give thanks to God always
> for you, brethren beloved by the Lord, because
> God from the beginning chose you for salvation
> through sanctification by the Spirit and belief
> in the truth (2 Thessalonians 2:13).

Notice the order of the clauses: chosen for salvation through sanctification and belief in the truth. Shouldn't belief in the gospel precede sanctification of the Spirit?

Here, sanctification comes before salvation because Paul isn't referring to the sanctification of believers but to the sanctification of sinners. This is the work of the Spirit in which He draws a circle around a lost person, sets him apart, and says in effect, "It's your time."

A college student, professing to be an atheist, once wrote to C. S. Lewis explaining that he had fallen in with some Christian students who were vigorously witnessing to him of their faith. Some of the things they said had unsettled his thinking; he was going through some great struggles. What did Dr. Lewis think? Lewis wrote back: "I think you are already in the meshes of the net—the Holy Spirit is after you. I doubt you will get away."

Salvation does not realize itself immediately. "The chariot of fire does not come down and snatch away one after another to glory."[2]

We find a similar thought in 1 Peter 1:2. Peter, addressing the pilgrims of the Dispersion, describes them as the "elect according to the foreknowledge of

God the Father, in sanctification of the Spirit, for obedience and sprinkling of the blood of Jesus Christ."

Again the order of the clauses is significant: "elect . . . in sanctification of the Spirit *for* obedience and sprinkling of the blood." We would assume that obedience and sprinkling of the blood would precede sanctification. But again, it appears that Peter is referring to a sanctification that brings about salvation, rather than a sanctification of the believer that follows salvation. Intercession plays a major role in this divine drama of preparation.

Here are some things that will help us as we pray for the lost. They are the context in which we intercede.

The Condition of the Sinner

1. The lost person is bound by the god of this world. Whether we evangelize through preaching or through praying, we must reckon with this fact. Let's look at some relevant passages.

> With gentleness he must correct his opponents, for God might grant them repentance that would lead them to a full knowledge of the truth, and they might recover their senses and *escape from the devil's trap in which they have been caught by him to do his will* (2 Timothy 2:25,26, WILLIAMS, emphasis added).

Men have been "taken alive" (the meaning of the Greek verb) by Satan, and as his captives they are slaves to his will. The only hope for them is that God may grant them repentance.

Paul writes:

> In which you once walked according to the course of this world, *according to the prince*

of the power of the air, the spirit who now
works in the sons of disobedience
(Ephesians 2:2, emphasis added).

The word translated "work" here is literally
"energizes," and is used elsewhere of the Holy Spirit's
activity in the believer. The unsaved person is ener-
gized by the spirit of the devil. Of course, a lost person
doesn't know that, and certainly would not admit it if
he did. He thinks he is free (that's part of his lostness),
but in truth his course of action is dictated by the prince
of the power of the air.

And in 1 John: "We know that we are of God,
and the whole world lies in the power of the evil one"
(5:19, NAS).

Forgive me if I sound like a dictionary, but the
Greek verb translated "lies" conveys the picture of a
mother cradling her baby in her arms and rocking it to
sleep. That is a vivid picture of the lost—cradled in the
arms of Satan, helplessly and hopelessly being lulled to
sleep.

Jesus said,

When a strong man well armed keeps guard
over his dwelling, *his property is secure.* But
when a man stronger than he attacks him and
overcomes him, he strips him of all his arms
on which he relied, and distributes his goods
as spoils (Luke 11:21,22, WILLIAMS, emphasis
added).

In this passage Jesus is answering the charge
that He casts out demons by Beelzebub, the ruler of
demons (Luke 11:14*ff.*). Two things are especially noteworthy in Jesus' reply:

First, men are described as the property of Satan, who stands guard over them lest they should escape; and

Second, before He can free the captives, Jesus must first deal with the captor, Satan, and disarm him. We will do well to keep that in mind.

In praying for a lost person, we are not forcing the person's will — we are *freeing* his will from the bondage of Satan.

2. The lost person is blinded to the gospel by the god of this world. Listen to Paul:

> But even if our gospel is veiled, it is veiled to those who are perishing, *whose minds the god of this age has blinded*, who do not believe, lest the light of the gospel of the glory of Christ, who is the image of God, should shine on them (2 Corinthians 4:3,4, emphasis added).

An unsaved person does not have the capacity to see himself as a lost sinner or to understand the gospel message. He has been blinded spiritually by Satan. Paul tells us that . . .

> the natural man does not receive the things of the Spirit of God, for they are foolishness to him; nor can he know them, because they are spiritually discerned (1 Corinthians 2:14).

No amount of human power, logic or argument can penetrate the darkness of the unsaved mind. We cannot explain the way of salvation simply enough for him to believe. The devil doesn't have to make a drunkard or a murderer of a person to keep him from being saved. He only has to keep him blind to the gospel of Christ.

3. Before any person can be saved, this (1) binding and (2) blinding of the devil must be overcome. There must be emancipation and enlightenment. As we saw earlier, Jesus first had to deal with the devil before He could free the captives.

This leads to the next truth we should understand in praying for the lost:

The Conquest of Satan

The devil is a defeated enemy. The New Testament clearly teaches that his defeat is twofold. **First,** it is *absolute*. We've already seen in Luke 11 that Jesus has bound the strong man, the devil. Another helpful passage is Hebrews 2:14,15:

> Since then the children share in flesh and blood, He Himself likewise also partook of the same, that through death He might render powerless him who had the power of death, that is, the devil; and might deliver those who through fear of death were subject to slavery all their lives (NAS).

Another passage says:

> He who sins is of the devil, for the devil has sinned from the beginning. For this purpose the Son of God was manifested, that He might destroy the works of the devil (1 John 3:8).

We read in Colossians that Christ has . . .

> cancelled out the certificate of debt consisting of decrees against us and which was hostile to us; and He has taken it out of the way, having nailed it to the cross. When He had disarmed the rulers and authorities, He made a public display of them, having triumphed over them through Him (2:14,15, NAS).

The language of this verse is taken from the victory march of the conquering Roman generals. After defeating an enemy, the victorious commander would chain the officers of the defeated army to his chariot and drag them back to Rome. He would send a runner ahead to announce to the city that the victory had been won, and the people would line the streets awaiting the spectacle.

By the way, do you know what that runner was doing? He was preaching. The same Greek word for a "herald," a proclaimer, an announcer, is used to describe preaching. The herald wasn't winning the victory, he was preaching and witnessing to a victory that already had been won.

Finally, the triumphant train entered the city, trumpets blaring, citizens cheering, garlands streaming, the conquering hero in his chariot drawn by magnificent white stallions. Trailing behind, chained to the chariot that was moving slightly faster than they could run, were the leaders of the defeated army — stumbling, falling, being dragged in the dust. The victor not only crushed his enemies, but he also made a public spectacle of them.

When Jesus died on the cross, He defeated Satan and all his thugs, and when He burst forth from the grave, He made a public spectacle of them. Satan's defeat is absolute.

Well, you may ask, *if that's so, then why do I have such a hard time with him? If the devil is chained, he either has a mighty long chain, or he's chained to me. Has anyone informed Satan of his defeat? He acts like he doesn't know it.* That's a good question, and there is a good answer.

Although Satan's defeat is absolute, for the time being — until God brings down the curtain on history — the **second** thing about his defeat is that it must be *appropriated*. This is true of everything God has done for us through Christ. What God has made available, we must appropriate.[3]

Look at Matthew 18:18:

> Truly I say to you, whatever you shall bind on earth shall have been bound in heaven; and whatever you loose on earth shall have been loosed in heaven (NAS).

We are to take our cue from heaven. Whatever has already been bound in heaven, we may bind on earth; whatever has already been loosed in heaven, we may loose on earth. We are to see things from heaven's viewpoint. Now, from heaven's viewpoint, has Satan been bound? Yes. From heaven's viewpoint, have slaves of Satan been loosed? Yes. Absolutely.

James provides a perfect illustration of this: "Therefore submit to God. Resist the devil and he will flee from you" (4:17).

Now, let's catch up with ourselves. So far we have said the unsaved are bound in slavery and blind to the gospel, and that it is the devil who has done this. Therefore, before any person can be saved, he must first be emancipated and enlightened. That is now possible because the devil, who has bound and blinded that person, has been defeated by Christ and rendered powerless. That brings us to . . .

The Cross of Christ

The atonement of Christ is the main pillar upon which intercession rests. In 1 John 2:1,2, we read:

My little children, these things I write to you,
that you may not sin. And if anyone sins, we
have an advocate with the Father, Jesus Christ
the righteous. And He Himself is the propitiation for our sins, and not for ours only but also
for the whole world.

Propitiation means "atoning sacrifice" or "cov-
ering." On the cross, Jesus covered our sins with His
blood, and not our sins only, but also those of the whole
world. He is the "Lamb of God, who takes away the sin
of the whole world!" (John 1:29) At this point someone
may say, "I believe in a limited atonement." Even so,
the principle is the same: The basis on which the elect
are saved is the atoning work of Christ. Men do not go
to hell because of their sins; they go because they reject
the atonement made by Christ:

For God did not send His Son into the world to
condemn the world, but that the world through
Him might be saved. He who believes in Him is
not condemned; but he who does not believe in
Him is condemned already *because he has not
believed in the name of the only begotten Son of
God* (John 3:17,18, emphasis added).

Why is the lost person condemned? Is it because
he steals, or curses, or gets drunk? No. He is not
condemned by what he has done, he is condemned by
what *he has not done*. He has not believed. In the
Revelation we find a picture of the final judgment of the
unsaved dead:

And I saw the dead, small and great, standing
before God, and books were opened. And
another book was opened, which is the Book
of Life. And the dead were judged according to
their works, by the things which were written
in the books. The sea gave up the dead who

> were in it, and Death and Hades delivered up
> the dead who were in them. And they were
> judged each one according to his works . . .
> And anyone *not found written in the Book of
> Life* was cast into the lake of fire (Revelation
> 20:13,15, emphasis added).

Observe that while the unsaved dead are judged
according to their works, they are not cast into the lake
of fire because of their works. The books of works are
opened to prove their need of salvation. They are cast
into the lake of fire because of what was *not written* in
the Book of Life—their names. Regardless of how bad
their record was, if their names had been written in the
Book of Life, they would have escaped the eternal
punishment.

Our right to pray for the lost is based on the fact
that Christ has already paid for their sin with His blood.
We are claiming what is rightly His.

One week in December when I was in seminary
in Ft. Worth, Texas, I preached at a Bible conference in
Florida. My wife and two-year-old son visited her parents in Arkansas. On my way home from Florida, I
picked them up in Arkansas and we arrived in Ft. Worth
on a freezing December afternoon. When we walked
into the house, we found that it was just as cold inside
as it was outside. It didn't take long to discover that our
gas had been cut off. With my little family standing
there shivering, I picked up the phone and called the
gas company and asked them what in the world was
going on. We were freezing to death, for heaven's sake.

A voice, as icy as the weather, replied, "Mr.
Dunn, you failed to pay last month's bill. We couldn't
get hold of you so we cut off your gas."

"But I paid it," I said.

"I'm sorry, but we have no record of any payment," the icy voice said. "You will have to come down to the office and pay the bill before we can turn the gas back on."

"Hang on a minute," I said. I put the phone down and began searching through my desk. Know what I was looking for? Right—the stub that had the gas company's stamp on it, the one that says PAID. And I found it. Grasping the proof of payment, I jerked up the receiver and told the icy voice to turn my gas back on, and do it now. And it was turned on.

When Christ poured out His blood, He paid the ransom for lost souls. When God raised Him from the grave the third day, He stamped the bill PAID IN FULL.

There will be times, as you pray for someone God has laid on your heart, when you will hear an icy voice saying, "You have no right to pray for him. He's my property. He belongs to me."

You can point to the proof of payment, the death and resurrection of Christ, and inform the icy voice that God has foreclosed on him (the devil) and bought up all his property.

When we pray for the lost in the name of Jesus, we claim what Jesus has already paid for with His blood. "Without any doubt, we may assure the conversion of those laid on our hearts by such praying. The prayer in Jesus' name drives the enemy off the battlefield of man's will and leaves him free to choose right."[4]

PART THREE

The Life
That Prays

Two
Conditions

Two things determine the answer to any prayer:
First, the prayer must be according to the will of God,
and **second**, the *pray-er* must be according to the will
of God.

Regardless of how earnestly we cry out to God
or how desperately we try to believe, any petition that
lies outside the will of God is doomed to failure. Prayer
doesn't get man's will done in heaven; it gets God's will
done on earth.

By pray-er, I mean the person who is praying. It
is the life that prays. As we have already seen, prayer
is as much *position* as it is petition. The prayer life rests
upon the pray-er's life, and if that life is weak, the entire
structure of the prayer life will collapse.

When we try to explain prayer, we raise as many questions as we answer. There is so much we can't know, but this much we do know: For an effective prayer life, *being* is more important than *doing*. If I am qualified to pray (we're going to discuss that in this chapter and in the two following), the Holy Spirit will see to it that I learn how.

On the other hand, if my life is wrong, even the Holy Spirit cannot make me an intercessor.

Living and Praying

Robert Murray McCheyene said, "What a man is in his prayer-closet is what he is." No Christian is greater than his prayer life, and his prayer life can be no greater than his personal life. I'm not saying we have to be super-saints or heroes of holiness, but we cannot divorce our living from our praying.

It is possible to preach without being right with God (I know—I've done it). Preaching is a person-to-person encounter. We can teach a Sunday school class or even witness to a lost person without being right with God. These are person-to-person encounters. Prayer, however, is a person-to-God encounter. It is an audience with one to whom all things are open and naked. We can't fake it with Him. What we are when we are alone with God is what we are. It is "the effective, fervent prayer of a righteous man" that avails much (James 5:16).

The psalmist said:

If I had cherished sin in my heart, the LORD would not have listened (Psalm 66:18, NIV).

To cherish iniquity means to look upon it with favor, to give it a place. The apostle John expressed it like this:

> And whatever we ask we receive from Him, because we keep His commandments and do those things that are pleasing in His sight (1 John 3:22).

Christ's Order of Worship

I speak in a different church every week and when I arrive on Sunday morning, the first thing I look for is the Order of Worship printed in the Sunday bulletin. They're all pretty much the same—an organ prelude, an anthem by the choir, followed by the invocation. I've often wondered how we would fare using the Lord's Order of Worship—which is:

> Therefore if you bring your gift to the altar, and there remember that your brother has something against you, leave your gift before the altar, and go your way. First, be reconciled to your brother, and then come and offer your gift (Matthew 5:23,24).

This is Christ's Order of Worship: First, be reconciled to your brother.

Imagine the chaos in church on Sunday morning if the members of the choir refused to sing until they made things right with their "brothers." What if the organist said, "I can't play yet; I've got to leave my gift here and first get right with my neighbor"? And what if the pastor said, "I can't offer my gift of preaching at this altar until I have first made things right with my deacons"?

Probably the Sunday morning worship wouldn't get underway until around four o'clock Monday afternoon, but when it did it would be something else.

What is the principle that Jesus gives us here? That the quality of the gift is determined by the quality of the giver. Or we can put it like this: *The acceptability of any act of worship is determined by the acceptability of the worshiper*. The gestures of worship are meaningless if the heart isn't right.

A Message From Micah

This is powerfully enforced by Micah the prophet. In the midst of a fiery controversy with the Lord, Israel says, "With what shall I come before the LORD, and bow myself before the high God?" (Micah 6:6a) And then they offer answers to their own question: "Shall I come before Him with burnt offerings, with calves of a year old?" (verse 6b) This is what is expected. But they go beyond that. "Will the Lord be pleased with thousands of rams or ten thousand rivers of oil?" (verse 7a) Only a king could bring such an offering. This is an extravagant offering. The Lord will surely be impressed.

The would-be-worshipers do not stop there. "Shall I give my firstborn for my transgression, the fruit of my body for the sin of my soul?" (verse 7b) These people are serious. Not even God would doubt the sincerity of such an extreme sacrifice. God is a tough negotiator, but Israel will meet His demands, whatever they are. Tell us what great thing to do, Lord!

Then Micah flings the answer at them:

He has showed you, O man, what is good; and
what does the LORD require of you but to do

justly, to love mercy, and to walk humbly with
your God? (Micah 6:8)

Not even the sacrifice of a firstborn child can
substitute for plain old honesty, kindness and humility.
The acceptability of the gift is determined by the acceptability of the giver.

When I stand to preach, God looks at my heart
before he listens to my sermon. If the heart is unaccep-
table, so is the sermon. The same is true of every activity
of the Christian life, and especially in the matter of
prayer.

Paul told Timothy he wanted . . .

> the men everywhere to offer prayer, lifting
> to heaven holy hands which are kept
> unstained by anger and dissensions
> (1 Timothy 2:8, WILLIAMS).

Lifting up the hands was one of the three basic
postures of praying among the Jews: kneeling, lying
prostrate, standing with hands lifted to heaven. The
emphasis here is not on *hands* but on *holy*. Paul could
just as well have said, "Kneel on holy knees." The
central concern here, as always in the New Testament,
is not the mechanics or gestures of worship, but the
attitude of the heart and the altitude of the life. Remember, it is the life that prays.

> Many think that they must, with their defec-
> tive spiritual life, work themselves up to pray
> more. They do not understand that only in
> proportion as the spiritual life is strengthened
> can the prayer life increase. Prayer and life are in-
> separably connected.
> —Andrew Murray

Learning
to Abide

I've been ambivalent about this section, THE
LIFE THAT PRAYS. I seriously considered saving it
until the last. As a young Christian I was easily daunted
by books on prayer because the authors usually jumped
immediately into the dreaded "Hindrances to Prayer."
By the time I got through that part I was too discouraged to read on. Some books would list as many as
twenty-five or thirty "hindrances" (those "sins" that
void our prayers). I was dismayed. I could never hope
to measure up—the mark was just too high.

So I thought I might say all the great and exciting things about prayer first, then when you were
hooked, give you the zinger.

Early on I spoke of prayer being the most intimidating word in the Christian vocabulary. It

shouldn't be. The biblical writers bend over backward to encourage us to pray. Prayer was God's idea; He wants us to pray far more than we want to. It is His delight to hear and answer.

Remember that as we go through this section. And if I end up discouraging and disheartening you, then I've presented it incorrectly. Don't pay any attention to what I said.

It is the life that prays . . . but what kind of life? Jesus puts it very simply in John 15:7:

> If you abide in Me, and My words abide in you,
> you will ask what you desire, and it shall be
> done for you.

Meet what should be the *normal* prayer life: "You will ask what you will, and it shall be done for you." This is from the same Bible that tells us we must pray "according to the will of God" (1 John 5:14). Jesus is speaking of a life of such quality, lived in such a dimension, where the will of the believer so harmonizes with the will of God that for the believer to "ask what he will" is synonymous with asking "according to His will."

This kind of praying flows from this kind of living: "Abide in Me, and My words abide in you." In this chapter and the next we will examine the "normal prayer life" pictured in these two statements.

A Life of Abiding

Admittedly, *abide* is not a word we use a great deal today. It smells musty, like old clothes packed away in a cedar chest. To appreciate what Jesus is saying, we need a little background.

As Jesus and His disciples made their way through the moonlit night from the upper room to the Garden of Gethsemane, Jesus continued His "upper room" discourse. Perhaps as they passed the Temple of Herod, He paused to gaze at the emblem adorning the monumental entrance, a vine. The vine was the national symbol, but Israel had become a "dead vine."

Jesus said, "I am the true vine." Actually Jesus said, "I am the vine, the true one." He is not one vine among others; he is the *true* vine, not necessarily as opposed to false, but, in the words of F. B. Meyer, "true in the sense of real, substantial, and enduring: the essential, as distinguished from the circumstantial, the eternal, as distinct from the temporary and transient."

In John 15, Jesus uses the figure of the true vine and its branches to describe His relationship with the disciples. I am to you, He tells the disciples, what the vine is to the branches. Here we must take time to read the first eight verses of the fifteenth chapter.

> I am the true vine, and My father is the vine-dresser. Every branch in Me that does not bear fruit He takes away; and every branch that bears fruit He prunes, that it may bear more fruit. You are already clean because of the word which I have spoken to you. Abide in Me, and I in you. As the branch cannot bear fruit of itself, unless it abides in the vine, neither can you, unless you abide in Me.

> I am the vine, you are the branches. He who abides in Me, and I in him, bears much fruit; for without Me you can do nothing. If anyone does not abide in me, he is cast forth as a branch and is withered; and they gather them and throw them into the fire, and they are burned. If you abide in Me, and My words abide

in you, you will ask what you desire and it shall
be done for you. By this is My Father glorified,
that you bear much fruit; so you will be My disciples (John 15:1-8).

Simply put, we are to be to Jesus what a branch
is to a vine. As the branch abides in the vine, we are to
abide in Jesus. *Abide* speaks of the union and communion between vine and branches. To abide in Jesus
is to live the life of a branch. What kind of life is that?
What does it mean for the branch to abide in the vine?

For one thing, it means that the branch must
accept the vine's purpose for its existence. That purpose
is stated in the second verse: "Every branch in Me that
does not bear fruit He [the Father] takes away."

Again, in verse 16:

You did not choose Me, but I chose you and appointed you that you should go and bear fruit,
and that your fruit should remain, that
whatever you ask the Father in My name He
may give you.

Obviously, the purpose of the branch is to bear
fruit. In itself it has no value. I love grapes, but I've
never eaten a grape branch. The fact is, apart from
bearing fruit, the branch cannot justify its existence.
The wood of the vine can't even be used for fuel. In Old
Testament times, people were instructed to bring sacrifices of wood to the Temple for the altar fires, any kind
of wood — except the wood of the vine. It's too soft to be
used for timber and there is little beauty in it. The
branches are so useless that when they are pruned from
the vine, they are piled in a heap and burned. The
branch is good for one thing only — bearing fruit.

And did you notice this? Jesus said, "Every branch in Me that *bears* fruit . . . " The branch does not produce the fruit; it bears the fruit. The vine produces the fruit—the branch is what God hangs the grapes on. The branch is just a grape rack.

This is what it means to abide—patiently resting in Christ, confident that He, the vine, will produce the fruit. A healthy branch will bear fruit. The responsibility of producing fruit is not upon us; that is the responsibility of Christ, the vine. Our part is to be healthy branches, living in union and communion with Him, so we can bear the fruit He produces.

Several years ago my wife and I attended the annual meeting of our denomination in Portland, Oregon. When our convention closed, we had a couple of free days before going home, so we looked for another convention to attend. As luck would have it, the F.P.A. (Fruitpickers of America) was holding its annual convention right there in Portland. I was surprised at the similarity of the two meetings. Like ours, the F.P.A. convention had lots of booths and exhibits, displaying the most advanced instruments for picking fruit, the latest techniques in fruitpicking, various sizes, shapes and colors of fruit baskets—things like that. There were a lot of speeches, too. We sat through them all. I especially liked the one on "Fruitpicking Burnout."

But the last speech was the best. It was delivered by the man who had led the convention in fruitpicking the previous year. The guy was a dynamic speaker and by the end of his message he had everyone on their feet, resolving they would pick more fruit than ever before. Inspired beyond their ability, the conventioneers grabbed baskets and rushed out to pick fruit.

We waited around. In a few hours the fruitpickers began drifting back in, passionless, joyless — and fruitless. Every basket was empty. Immediately a task force was formed to discover why, with the latest methods and the finest tools, their fruitpicking crusade flopped. We couldn't stay around for the official report, but we heard about it sometime later. It seemed they had devoted all their time and energy to fruitpicking and none to fruit*bearing*. They forgot that you have to *bear* fruit before you can pick it.

So here is the first essential in branch life: acknowledging that the purpose for which Christ saved us is fruitbearing. As the vine manifests its life through the branch, so Jesus manifests His life through us. The Christian is, among other things — a Christ-like life. *Fruit is the outward expression of the inward nature.*

Some people can look at a leaf and tell you what kind of tree it is. I can't do that. I must see the fruit. When I see an apple growing on a tree, I'm pretty sure it's an apple tree. The apple is the outward expression of the inward nature. Apple in nature, apple in fruit.

In the same way, Christ is the inward nature of the Christian, and if we are in union and communion with Him we will bear fruit. Our part is to abide.

Fruit, More Fruit, Much Fruit

A subtle progression of fruitlessness is found in Jesus' words. In the second verse, He speaks of a branch that *bears* fruit, then is pruned to bear *more* fruit. Finally, in verse five, Jesus says that "he who abides in Me, and I in Him, bears *much* fruit." This progression should not be overlooked, for just as the vinedresser wants his vine to produce more and more fruit, Jesus wants us to do the same. You and I can bear more fruit than we are bearing. We have not reached our potential, and the Vinedresser intends that we should.

How does He do that? Does He make us more fruitful by adding more branches? That seems to be the logical answer.

As a pastor, I have done that, thinking, *If we add more activities, we'll grow more fruit*—we only grew weary. We are like the little boy who played cowboys and Indians all day, riding his stick horse all over the neighborhood. That night when his father asked him why he was so tired, the boy said, "Real cowboys have real horses, but I have to do my own galloping."

No wonder we grow weary in well doing—we do our own galloping. It is not *more* branches that make the vine more fruitful; it is *healthier* branches.

One summer at our farm in Arkansas I noticed a tree standing alone in a field. One side of the tree was lush with green leaves, but on the other side the leaves were dead. It was as though someone had drawn a straight line from the top of the tree to the bottom and divided it—one half alive, one half dead.

I was back for Thanksgiving. Winter was coming and the trees were bare; everywhere you went you walked on a carpet of fallen leaves. I saw again the lone tree in the field. It was still divided, half dead, half alive—but only one side of the tree was bare. On the living side the leaves had fallen off, leaving the branches deserted, but the other half, the dead half, was heavy with brown, brittle leaves. Have you ever noticed that dead leaves fall off living trees, but dead leaves on dead trees do not? Why is that?

The truth is, dead leaves don't *fall* off living trees — they are *pushed* off. It is the sap, the life of the tree, moving and dropping, that pushes the dead leaves off to make room for the new leaves of spring. Isn't it neat the way God arranged it? We don't have to climb the trees each autumn to pull off the dead leaves, and then climb them again in the spring to attach new ones. The trees take care of that themselves. All we do is make certain they are healthy so the life of the tree flows unhindered through the branches.

Available to His Purpose

Having accepted the Vine's purpose for my life, I now must make myself *available to that purpose*.

Have you ever watched a branch? It's not exactly exciting. It just sits there, doing nothing but resting in its appointed place, never isolated from its source of life. It "abides."

I'm not suggesting that abiding in Christ means we sit down and do nothing. On a number of occasions in the Old Testament God told the people to "stand still," but I don't see any of them standing still. They were pretty active folk. Their standing "still" didn't mean standing around.

In the same way, abiding in Christ is not idling in Christ. Jesus was able to do what He did because He was constantly abiding in the Father, yet no one could accuse Jesus of idleness or passivity. The writer of Hebrews says that "he who has entered in His [God's] rest has himself also ceased from his works as God did from His" (Hebrews 4:10). He doesn't say that he ceased from work, just from *his own works*. Now he is doing the works of God.

The branch places itself at the disposal of the vine, for the vine to do with as it pleases. We do the same, saying, "Lord, here is my life. It's Yours to do with as You please. I'm available."

I remember speaking at Campus Crusade for Christ's staff training at Ft. Collins, Colorado. In fact, I spoke on this very theme. One afternoon while I was visiting with several staffers, one said to me, "I really don't want to be here. I don't have the time."

I said, "That's like the branch saying to the vine, 'I don't have time to abide in the vine—I'm too busy bearing fruit.'"

A Talk With a Water Faucet

There was a period in my Christian walk (and probably in yours, too) when I would come to the end of the day wondering if I had done enough for Christ. Should I have done more? Could I have done more? How much was enough, anyway? The Accuser would add fuel to my self-condemnation by reminding me of the many things I had left undone. Consequently, much of my at-the-close-of-the-day praying went something like this: "Lord, forgive me. I know I didn't do all I should have today. Help me to do more tomorrow."

That was before I talked with the water faucet. One day, walking through the kitchen, I noticed the water faucet seemed down in the dumps. I stopped and said, "Hey, Faucet, what's wrong? You look depressed."

"Yes, Master, I am."

"Why so?"

Faucet looked down. "I failed you. I'm sorry."

"Failed me? How?"

"Well, sir, I've seen you pass by a dozen times today and I haven't done anything for you. I haven't washed your hands; I haven't quenched your thirst; I haven't done anything. Oh, a couple of times I tried to turn myself on, but I was only able to squeeze out a couple of drops. It didn't amount to much. I'm sorry."

I patted his shiny chrome handle. "You silly water faucet. You're right. I have passed by you a dozen times today and you haven't done anything for me. You haven't turned on once today—that's my business. If I had wanted to wash my hands or take a drink, I would have turned you on. I don't want you turning yourself on—all you will do is waste water and make a mess."

I looked Faucet straight in the nozzle and said, "Listen to me. Every time I walked by today, I knew you were here. I knew that if I wanted to use you, all I had to do was touch you and you would respond. I don't measure your faithfulness by how much water you dispense in a day. I judge you by your *availability*. You have been faithful to me today, Faucet, because you have been available to me. I'm proud of you."

I don't know if that little talk helped Faucet or not, but it did me a lot of good. It reminded me that God does not judge me by the achievement of my hand, but by the ambition of my heart. As God said to David, I believe He says to us: "You did well in that it was in your heart" (2 Chronicles 6:8).

Remember the beautiful picture Christ gives us in the Gospel of John? "If any man is thirsty, let him come to Me and drink. . . . From his innermost being shall flow rivers of living water" (John 7:37,38, NASB). *You provide the riverbed and I'll provide the river.* That's availability.

His Words, Our Will

It's easy for our religion to become just a matter of words, to take the Bible literally but not seriously.

One of the charges God brought against His people through the prophet Hosea was that they treated His Word as a stranger (Hosea 8:12). The stranger was not at home in Israel; he had no permanent dwelling place there. He was allowed to live there but he had no voice in the land. Being a stranger, he had no say-so in the affairs of Israel. He possessed no vote. Whatever opinion he might have about important issues was ignored.

His Words Abiding in Us: Controlled by the Word

The Word of God occupies a strategic position in the life that can pray. Jesus said, "If you abide in Me, *and My words abide in you,* you will ask what you desire, and it shall be done for you" (John 15:7, emphasis added). The word *abide* is a strong one and means "to settle down permanently, to be at home in." Jesus means that His words must have a home in our hearts. Unfortunately, instead of a home for the Word of God, many of us have made our hearts a hotel, and check-out time is 12 noon on Sunday.

Years ago I heard of an evangelist who used to go from village to village holding revival meetings. In every town the first thing he did was organize a "shouting committee" that would sit on a pew in the back of the church and take down the names of everyone who shouted during the services. The next day they would go around town, checking up on the shouters, and if they found one with a bad reputation, they told him to stop shouting in the meetings.

And then there was the big fellow in one of my meetings who, when asked by a friend why he didn't have a Bible, replied, "Oh, I just came to shout."

"Just coming to shout" would not have set well with the apostle John. He said,

> Now by this we know that we know Him, if
> we keep His commandments. He who says,
> "I know Him," and does not keep His com-
> mandments is a liar and the truth is not in
> him (1 John 2:3,4).

John sounds like a member of the shouting committee. He uses the phrase, "He who says," over and over, as if he had in mind a particular person, perhaps someone who professed to know Jesus but whose life denied it.

These are hard words. If someone says he knows Jesus but does not keep His commandments, he is a liar. Period. This sounds like sinless perfection, but it isn't. No one, not even John, lives a faultless life.

A Watchful Eye

The key to understanding these verses is the word *keep* which means to be vigilant, to keep a watchful eye on something. It was used of ancient seamen who each kept a watchful, vigilant eye on the stars, and they sailed by them accordingly.

It took me three trips to England before I got up enough nerve to drive a car there. A friend loaned us his for two weeks—if he was willing to risk his car, so was I. Some of the highway signs in England are different from those in the States. For instance, "No Waiting on the Verge" is England's way of saying, "No Curbside Parking." We bought a book that paralleled the English signs and the American signs. My wife navigated. With the book open in her lap, she translated the signs and kept saying, "Think left, think left."

I've never been more vigilant. I kept a watchful eye on the signs and regulated my driving accordingly. That is what John is saying. A person who really knows Jesus does not have a nonchalant attitude toward His commandments.

A Frame of Reference

Keeping His commandments means we have a God-reference to life. God and His Word are taken into account; we bring everything under the judgment of God's Word. We do not make decisions without taking into account what is pleasing to Him (cf. 1 John 3:22). He is our frame of reference.

His Words Abiding in Us: Cleansed by His Word

"I am the true vine," said Jesus . . .

and My Father is the vinedresser. Every branch in Me that does not bear fruit he takes away; and every branch that bears fruit He prunes, that it may bear more fruit (John 15:1,2).

Earlier I called attention to the progression of fruitfulness in this passage. In verse two, the branch *bears* fruit, then it bears *more* fruit, and in verse five, it bears *much* fruit. The life that prays is not static; it is dynamic, living, growing, increasing.

Question: How does God, the Vinedresser, bring us from simply bearing fruit to bearing much fruit? As I mentioned earlier, not by adding branches, but by making the branches healthier. And, sorry about that, the branches are made healthier by pruning.

If you have watched someone prune a tree or a vine, you know that the vinedresser is merciless in his cutting. We have three trees in our backyard that have been denuded by vicious pruning—they look awful. The pruning process is ruthless. We would never guess that what appears to be cruelty on the part of the vine-dresser is really tenderness.

Sometimes we misjudge the Vinedresser. We may be resting in our appointed place, abiding in the vine, bearing good fruit, when suddenly heavy steps are heard entering the vineyard. Instantly, the word comes through the grapevine: The Vinedresser has come, and

He's carrying pruning shears. And then He's standing in front of you, and for no reason at all, without a word of explanation, He starts clipping away some of your best wood. Nearby vines try to encourage you: It will be all right, they say; it's for your own good, they say; you will live through it, they say. But you know you won't. You can't understand the cruelty of the Vinedresser — this, after you won the Most Fruitful Branch of the Year award.

Nevertheless, if you're a branch, pruning goes with the territory; it's an occupational hazard. Branches are instruments, not ornaments. The word here for "prune" is translated "cleanse," which, when used in reference to the vine, means "to prune by the removal of superfluous wood."

The Father does the pruning and the Word of God is His shears (John 15:3). Everything in the branch that diverts the vital power from producing fruit is cut away. He prunes all the bad and much of the good. Even the most immature branch can understand having the bad cut off, but having so much good wood cut away seems reckless and wasteful, as though the Vinedresser enjoyed pruning, enjoyed our pain. It's almost a crime — that beautiful wood, those lovely leaves, all going to waste.

Yet the Lord of the vineyard is cutting away only useless wood. It may be beautiful, but it takes up room and burns precious fuel that in another branch would produce luscious grapes.

We do not have to be great backsliders to be unfruitful; we simply sometimes get entangled in many "good" activities. The biggest threat to the best is not the bad, but the good — good things that clutter our lives so there is no room to grow, things that drain so much of our energy there is nothing left for bearing fruit. We are so busy *doing* that there is no time to *be*. There is too much wood.

One Thing Needed

This is graphically illustrated by an incident in the lives of Mary and Martha. Practically every time you see Martha, she's in the kitchen; that girl loved to cook. But she had trouble getting her sister Mary to help her. Mary had other interests. The story is told in Luke 10:38-42:

> Now it happened as they went that He entered a certain village; and a certain woman named Martha welcomed Him into her house. And she had a sister called Mary, who also sat at Jesus' feet and heard His word. But Martha was distracted with much serving, and she approached Him and said, "Lord, do You not care that my sister has left me to serve alone? Therefore tell her to help me."

Let's pause for a minute. At this point, whose side are you on? Myself, I side with Martha. It's not fair that she must do everything by herself. Mary's just lazy.

Now we'll listen to Jesus' opinion:

> And Jesus answered and said to her, "Martha, Martha, you are worried and troubled about many things. But one thing is needed, and Mary has chosen that good part, which will not be taken away from her."

That's a surprise. Just *one* thing needed? Are we ready for this—out of the many things we do, good things, important things, hundreds of things, only *one* is needed? That's right, just one. Martha was so dis-

tracted by her busyness that she didn't recognize it.
Jesus contrasted Martha's "many things" to Mary's
"one thing." Martha was so busy serving the Lord she
didn't have time to enjoy His presence.

Martha's service to Christ should have brought
joy and peace to her heart but instead it brought
anxiety, worry and anger. Her well-intended labor suc-
ceeded only in breaking the harmony between her and
her sister, and it cast a gloom over the entire affair.
Does that sound familiar?

There is only one thing needed because Jesus
will survive if Martha doesn't feed Him. He could turn
every stone into bread, if necessary.

> If I were hungry, I would not tell you," says
> the LORD. "For the world is Mine, and all its
> fullness" (Psalm 50:12).

Yes, Jesus will survive if Martha doesn't feed
Him, *but Martha won't survive if Jesus doesn't feed her.*
I've seen many successful Christians "die on the vine"
because they were so busy serving Christ they had no
time to sit at His table and feast on His Word.

Mary had "chosen that good part." That's a
culinary term, the parlance of the kitchen. It was the
choice piece, the portion reserved for the guest of honor
at the feast. While Martha thought she was preparing
the choice portion for Jesus, He gave it to Mary.

Read It and Reap

Have you spent time sitting at the feet of Jesus,
enjoying His presence, feasting on His Word? Nothing,
not even prayer, can take the place of faithful reading
and diligent study of the Bible. Here are some practical

suggestions to help you read it and reap the good portion.

1. Read the Bible *regularly.* Don't let the sun set on a day in which you have not spent time alone with God before the open Word. It's important to gather fresh manna every day.

2. Read the Bible *alertly.* Choose a time when your mind is fresh and awake. Don't give God the drowsy dregs of a busy day.

3. Read the Bible *systematically.* If you read Leviticus 11:3, then Revelation 5:7, then Psalm 15:4, don't blame the Bible if you come away confused. Pick out a book (Philippians, for example), start with chapter one, verse one, word one, and read through the book. You will be surprised at how much sense the Bible makes when it is read sensibly.

4. Read the Bible with *variety.* Try using different translations. I recommend *Charles B. Williams', The New Testament in the Language of the People, The New American Standard Version, The New International Version, The Revised English Bible* and *The Revised Standard Version.*

5 Read the Bible *prayerfully.* Ask God to give you something to live by that day. Turn the verses into prayers and praises.

6. Read the Bible *expectantly.* Approach your Bible study expecting God to meet you and speak to you through His Word.

7. Read the Bible *obediently.* Unless it is obeyed, the Bible will eventually end up on a shelf, closed. Revelation demands response. Obedience keeps the daily devotion from becoming an empty ritual.

The life that prays is the life in which "the word of Christ dwells in [us] richly" (Colossians 3:16).

Fasting: A Biblical Survey

When I was nine, our family moved into a new house. On the kitchen wall above the stove, painted in red script, was this motto: "The Way to a Man's Heart Is Through His Stomach." Though today some might scorn that as a sexist statement, the truth of it has been confirmed a million times over. As a matter of fact, the devil has been operating under that same motto for thousands of years. He discovered long ago that the way to a man's heart is through his physical appetites.

The first temptation hurled at man was related to his physical appetite:

> When the woman saw that the tree was good
> for food, she took from its fruit and ate; and
> she gave to her husband with her, and he ate
> (Genesis 3:6).

Since that first garden experience, there has been a steady stream of temptation aimed at the appetite. After a mighty deliverance from the judgment of God, Noah abused his physical appetite and got drunk. Isaac favored Esau above Jacob because Esau was a hunter and provided his father with plenty of good meat. Unfortunately, Esau allowed his stomach to overrule his good sense and sold his birthright for a bowl of chili.

Notice how Paul describes in 1 Corinthians 10:7 the idolatry of Israel after their escape from Egypt. If I had been called upon to report the incident, I think I would have mentioned the golden calf and the other shenanigans that took place. Not Paul. He states it simply: "The people sat down to eat and drink, and stood up to play." He knew the real issue was not the calf but the uncontrolled physical appetite.

In the wilderness temptation of Jesus, the devil aimed his first barrage at the physical appetite of the Son of Man: "If you are the Son of God, command that these stones become bread" (Matthew 4:3). Later, Paul warned the Philippians to steer clear of people "whose god is their appetite" (Philippians 3:19).

Prominence of Fasting in the Old Testament

In these passages and many others, the Bible reveals a pronounced relationship between a person's spiritual status and his physical appetite. A lack of discipline here is symptomatic of a lack of discipline in other areas of the life. Perhaps this is why the Bible has so much to say about fasting.

Many Christians are surprised to discover the prominence of fasting in the Bible. Most of us probably have never seriously considered fasting as a part of Christian living. Because we associate it with fanatical or legalistic religions, we have practically dismissed it as being irrelevant to twentieth-century Christianity. But no serious study of the deeper truths of intercession can afford to overlook fasting or relegate it to an unimportant status. So a quick survey is in order.

After his encounter with Jezebel, Elijah, in desperate need of personal revival, went to Mt. Horeb where he fasted for forty days (1 Kings 19:8).

Esther's fast played an important role in the deliverance she obtained for her people (Esther 4:16).

David fasted when his baby was stricken (2 Samuel 12:16). Daniel fasted and prayed until God's heavenly messenger broke through enemy lines to bring Daniel an answer from the throne of God (Daniel 10:3). Both Ezra and Nehemiah proclaimed fasts during national crises (Ezra 8:21; Nehemiah 1:4).

Fasting in the New Testament

Fasting is not confined to the Old Testament. In Luke 2:37 it is recorded of Anna, the prophetess, that she "never left the temple, serving night and day with fastings and prayers." John the Baptist fasted and taught his disciples to do likewise.

Jesus practiced fasting and made it clear that He expected His followers to do the same. Take the sixth chapter of Matthew, for example. In this chapter, Jesus warns His disciples about doing the right thing for the wrong motive. The Christian life, He says, is fragile; handle it with care. Make certain your motives are pure. To illustrate His point He takes three representative religious practices and shows how these can be performed for the praise of men rather than for the praise of God.

The three He mentions are almsgiving, prayer and fasting. Note the wording in verse 16: "Whenever you fast . . . "; and again in verse 17: "But you, when you fast . . . " *Whenever . . . when.* Jesus did not say, *if* you fast, but *when* you fast. It was expected that His disciples would fast. As a matter of fact, Jesus here makes fasting just as much a religious duty as almsgiving and prayer. No modern Christian would claim that almsgiving (acts of charity) and prayer are out of date. And neither is fasting. Jesus placed it on the same plane with prayer and acts of charity.

In Matthew 9:14,15, we find:

> Then the disciples of John came to Him, saying, "Why do we and the Pharisees fast, but your disciples do not fast?" And Jesus said to them, "The attendants of the bridegroom cannot mourn as long as the bridegroom is with them, can they? But the days will come when the bridegroom is taken away from them, and then they will fast."

While Jesus was physically present with His disciples they had no need to fast. The time for fasting would come when Jesus was taken out of the world. Today, as we still await the return of the bridegroom, there are times when fasting is called for.

Immediately following his conversion, the apostle Paul fasted for three days (Acts 9:9). Fasting was a permanent part of his life and ministry. When writing to the Corinthians of his own personal ministry, he says:

> But in everything commending ourselves as
> servants of God, in much endurance, in afflic-
> tions, in hardships, in distresses, in stripes, in
> imprisonments, in tumults, in labors, in watch-
> ings, in *fastings* (2 Corinthians 6:5, emphasis
> added).

Then again in 2 Corinthians 11:27: "I have been
in labor and hardship, through many sleepless nights,
in hunger and thirst, often without food [Greek: fast-
ing], in cold and exposure."

The book of Acts shows that fasting was a vital
part of the young church's life:

> And while they were ministering to the Lord
> and fasting, the Holy Spirit said, "Set apart
> Barnabas and Saul for the work to which I have
> called them." Then when they had fasted and
> prayed and laid their hands on them, they sent
> them away (Acts 13:2,3, RSV).

Acts 14:23 describes the missionary ministry of
Paul and Barnabas in strengthening the newly formed
congregations:

> When they had appointed elders for them in
> every church, having prayed with fasting, they
> commended them to the Lord in whom they
> had believed (RSV).

A Definition of Fasting

The Hebrew word means "to cover the mouth,"
and the Greek words mean simply, "not to eat," but
fasting is much more than going hungry. As a matter
of fact, fasting isn't confined to food and water, though
that is its primary expression. By mutual agreement, a
husband and wife may "fast" from sexual relations in

order to devote themselves fully to prayer (1 Corinthians 7:5).

Let me offer this definition: *Fasting is the voluntary abstinence of satisfaction from certain physical appetites, for spiritual reasons.* Most often, fasting is abstaining from food and drink, though it could be any number of things.

Different Kinds of Fasts

The Bible speaks of different kinds of fasts. Some fasts are *public*. After hearing the prophetic message of Jonah, the king of Ninevah proclaimed a fast throughout the city, denying even the animals food and water (Jonah 3:5-10). The prophet Joel called for a nationwide fast for the purpose of seeking the Lord for mercy and revival (Joel 1:14).

Much of our fasting is to be *private*. In Matthew 6:16-18, Jesus warns us against dressing or behaving in a manner that would cause men to know we are fasting. A few years ago I received a church newsletter carrying this headline: "Pastor Ends Forty-Day Fast." I thought at the time that whatever spiritual gains he made during the fast, he may have lost by publicizing it. I don't know. It would be mighty hard to fast for forty days and not tell somebody about it.

How Long Does a Fast Last?

The Bible records fasts of one day, three days, seven days, twenty-one days and forty days. There is no fixed time limit. Jesus was "led of the Spirit" to fast for forty days (Matthew 4:1,2), and we must allow the Holy Spirit to lead us in the matter of length. Normally, a

Christian who is sensitive enough to the Spirit to start a fast will be sensitive enough to know when to stop.

Degrees of Fasting

One of the most interesting features of fasting in the Bible is the varying degrees of a fast. Some went without food and water, others without food, still others abstained only from wine and pleasant bread. I think it will be helpful to categorize these differing degrees.

There is the *extreme fast* in which no food or drink is taken. Paul's fast in Acts 9:9 was an extreme fast. Moses' fast while receiving the law from God falls into this category. He went without food and drink for forty days – an extremely difficult task.

In a *normal fast* one abstains from food but does drink water. This is the usual method of fasting. Elijah's fast was probably a normal fast, for the Bible speaks only of his going without food (1 Kings 19:8). It is thought that Jesus drank water during His forty-day fast since the Gospel accounts mention only His hunger, not any thirst.

Then there is the *partial fast*. This is described in Daniel 10:3: "I did not eat any tasty food, nor did meat or wine enter my mouth, nor did I use ointment at all, until the entire three weeks were completed."

Why Fast?

Let me emphasize this important point: In the Bible, the purpose of fasting is always *spiritual,* to attain some spiritual end. While fasting can be an aid to health in purifying the body and taking off weight, this is not fasting in the biblical sense. For me, it is true that when I feel God leading me to fast for some reason,

I have no trouble doing it. The hunger barely bothers me. But when I fast to lose weight, it is war on every front.

Fasting for Spiritual Discipline

It appears from the Scripture that God's original purpose in commanding the people to fast was for self-abasement and self-humbling. In Psalm 35:13, David says, "But as for me, when they were sick, my clothing was sackcloth: I humbled my soul with fasting."

Again, in Psalm 69:10, he says, "When I wept and chastened my soul with fasting, that was my reproach." This is a beautiful thought: *Fasting is the weeping of the soul.*

Then in Psalm 109:24, "My knees are weak through fasting; and my flesh faileth of fatness."

In Ezra 8:21, we read, "Then I proclaimed a fast there at the river Ahava, that we might humble ourselves before our God" (NASB).

One of the things God desires most from His people is self-humbling. We sometimes pray, "Lord, make me humble." But I don't think that's a biblical prayer. I find nowhere in the Bible where God is supposed to humble us. He may humiliate us, but we have to humble ourselves. That's our responsibility. And I repeat: Self-humbling delights the heart of God and makes it possible for Him to bless us. The apostle Peter declares,

> You younger men, likewise, be subject to your elders, and all of you, clothe yourselves with humility toward one another, for *God is opposed to the proud, but gives grace to the*

humble. Humble yourselves, therefore, under
the mighty hand of God, that He may exalt you
at the proper time (1 Peter 5:5,6, NASB, emphasis added).

Jesus' call to discipleship is a call to deny self in
order that we may discover our all in Him. Fasting is a
perfect expression of godly sorrow and repentance because genuine sorrow overrides our desire for food.
Thus, fasting becomes an outward expression of our
inner repentance.

Remember the relation between physical appetite and spiritual discipline. The sin of Sodom was
linked with a "surfeit of food." Of Israel, God said,
"When I fed them to the full, they committed adultery."
When the appetite for food and drink is abused, the life
is laid open to attacks in other areas. The opposite is
also true: When the physical appetites are brought
under control, the spiritual life is strengthened and
reinforced. I can't emphasize this too strongly. *Fasting
is a spiritual discipline that helps subdue the body and
master the appetite.*

Fasting as a Spiritual Companion

Fasting is rarely practiced alone. It is always
linked with another spiritual activity. Nowhere are we
commanded to fast only, but to fast *and* pray, to put on
sackcloth and ashes (signs of godly sorrow and repentance) *and* fast, to seek the Lord *with* fasting, or to
minister to the Lord *with* fasting.

Fasting creates an atmosphere in which these
other spiritual exercises can be done more effectively;
they flourish in a fasting climate. Fasting is the perfect
environment for prayer and seeking the Lord. With

fasting we detach ourselves from the earth, and with prayer we attach ourselves to heaven. It enables us to abandon ourselves more completely to God during times of intense spiritual devotion. Along with many others, I have found that during seasons of fasting, I have more liberty in prayer, more enlightenment in Bible study, and a deeper sense of God's presence.

Fasting under the Spirit's leadership heightens our spiritual understanding and makes us more sensitive to the things of God. Jesus' forty-day fast in the wilderness prepared Him for the satanic onslaught He had to face. It was through prayer and fasting that Daniel received a revelation from God. As the church at Antioch was ministering to the Lord and fasting, the Holy Spirit revealed to them His plan for Paul and Barnabas. It was in an atmosphere of prayer and fasting that Paul and Barnabas appointed elders to the church and commended them to the Lord. In Deuteronomy 9:9,10, Moses tells us that he received the law in a climate of fasting and waiting.

Fasting for Divine Protection

An example of fasting for deliverance and protection is found in Ezra 8:21-23:

> Then I proclaimed a fast there at the river Ahava, that we might humble ourselves before our God *to seek from Him a safe journey for us, our little ones, and all our possessions.* For I was ashamed to request from the king troops and horsemen to protect us from the enemy on the way, because we had said to the king, "The hand of our God is favorably disposed to all who seek Him, but His power and His anger are against all those who forsake Him." So we

fasted and sought our God concerning this matter, and He listened to our entreaty (NASB, emphasis added).

This is a beautiful story. The people are about
to begin a four-month march from Babylon to Jerusalem, a journey that will take them through a stony
desert infested with bands of thieves. The king offered
his soldiers to accompany Ezra and his people, but Ezra
declined, boasting that their God was all the protection
they needed.

It's easy to talk about trusting God when you
are safely behind the walls of Babylon. It's another
story when you find yourself in the midst of danger
without the strong arm of the flesh to support you. And
right here is where many Christians give the world
cause to mock. Thank God, when the chips were down,
Ezra didn't run to the world for help. He was ashamed
to. Though Ezra was walking in human flesh, he did not
war with the weapons of the flesh, but proclaimed a fast
and sought the Lord, and the Lord delivered them.

Second Chronicles 20 records one of the
strangest battles ever fought (see chapter 4). King
Jehoshaphat was facing an attack from an overwhelm-
ing Syrian army. He had enough sense to be afraid and
"turned his attention to seek the Lord; and proclaimed
a fast throughout all Judah" (2 Chronicles 20:3, NASB),
and then he cried to the Lord,

> O our God, wilt Thou not judge them? For we
> are powerless before this great multitude who
> are coming against us; nor do we know what to
> do, but our eyes are on Thee (verse 12).

While they were fasting and praying, God gave
them the battle plan. And what a plan it was—the king

was to send the music makers out before the fighting troops. Those who were appointed to sing to the Lord and praise Him went out before the army, and "when they began singing and praising, the Lord set ambushes against the sons of Ammon, Moab and Mount Seir who had come against Judah; so they were routed" (verse 22). By the way, that's a great description of fasting—"but our eyes are on Thee."

Could it be that in our day God is waiting to reveal His battle plan that would deliver us from our enemies? Is He waiting for another Jehoshaphat to seek the Lord and proclaim a fast throughout the land?

Fasting to Avert God's Wrath

God had spoken. In forty days Ninevah would be destroyed. So certain was this judgment that when it was averted, Jonah, the prophetic proclaimer of that advancing doom, became angry with the Lord and pleaded to die. But the king of that wicked city repented in sackcloth and ashes and declared a fast in the city. And the Bible says . . .

> When God saw their deeds, that they turned from their wicked ways, then God relented concerning the calamity which He had declared He would bring upon them. And He did not do it (Jonah 3:10, NASB).

Deliverance Through Intercession and Fasting

The examples we've looked at so far have been, for the most part, examples of personal deliverance. But God uses intercession and fasting to bring about the deliverance of *others* also. Let me cite three incidents.

In Ezra 10:6, we read:

> Then Ezra rose from before the house of God
> and went into the chamber of Jehohanan the
> son of Eliashib. Although he went there, he
> did not eat bread, nor drink water, for he was
> mourning over the unfaithfulness of the exiles
> (NASB).

While in exile the people had broken God's commandment by intermarrying, and Ezra's grief over their sin expressed itself through fasting. The result was that the people confessed their sin and abandoned the practice of intermarriage.

Another example of intercession and fasting is found in the first chapter of Nehemiah. This man of God prays for his backslidden people:

> Now it came about when I heard these words, I
> sat down and wept and mourned for days; and I
> was fasting and praying before the God of
> heaven. And I said, "I beseech Thee, O LORD
> God of heaven . . . let Thine ear now be atten-
> tive and Thine eyes open to hear the prayer of
> Thy servant which I am praying before Thee
> now, day and night, on behalf of the sons of Is-
> rael Thy servants, confessing the sins of the
> sons of Israel which we have sinned against
> Thee; I and my father's house have sinned"
> (Nehemiah 1:4-6, NASB).

No greater illustration of delivering others through prayer and fasting exists than that of Moses. Perhaps he more than any other (outside of Jesus) knew what it meant to stand in the gap between a holy God and a sinful people. Before he died, Moses laid down the reins and reminded Israel of his intercession for them:

> And I fell down before the LORD, as at the first,
> forty days and nights; I neither ate bread nor
> drank water, because of all your sin which you
> had committed in doing what was evil in the
> sight of the LORD to provoke Him to anger. For
> I was afraid of the anger and hot displeasure
> with which the LORD was wrathful against you
> in order to destroy you *but the LORD listened to
> me that time also.* And the LORD was angry
> enough with Aaron to destroy him; *so I also
> prayed for Aaron at the same time* (Deuter-
> onomy 9:18-20, NASB, emphasis added).

Think of it: Just *one* man, paying the price in fasting and intercession, and an entire nation was delivered from judgment. Do we even dare guess what might take place in our homes and schools and churches, *in our world,* if Christians awakened to their right and responsibility to wield such power through prayer and fasting? Can you envision the unending procession of liberated lives streaming out of darkness into the Kingdom of Light? Can you hear the happy cries of mothers and fathers saturating the heavens as wayward sons and daughters come to Jesus? Can you see Satan cower in defeat as hundreds of intercessors invade his citadel and set free the captives of sin?

The Rewards of Fasting

Jesus said,

> But you, when you fast, anoint your head, and
> wash your face so that you may not be seen fast-
> ing by men, but by your Father who is in
> secret; and your Father who sees in secret will
> repay you (Matthew 6:17,18, NASB).

Jesus did not consider rewards too low a motive to mention, and along with acts of charity and prayer,

He promised a reward would be given to those who fasted in the proper spirit. In the sixteenth verse He mentions the reward of those who fast in order to impress others with their piety: "Truly I say to you, they have their reward in full" (NASB).

The word Jesus uses for reward in verse 16 is different from the one used in verse 18. The word used to describe the reward of the hypocrite implies an *immediate reward* and a *reward paid in full.* In other words, "What you see is what you get." But the word Jesus uses to describe the reward given in response to the right spirit suggests a restoration over a period of time. The rewards of fasting are like dividends from blue chip stock. Day after day, God continues to unfold for you and others the rewards of fasting.

PART FOUR

The God
Who Hears

The Prayer God Always Answers

Some time ago a missionary told me about a letter he received from a little girl whose Sunday school class had been writing to foreign missionaries. Evidently their teacher had told them real live missionaries were very busy and might not have time to answer their letters, for the one he received said simply:

Dear Rev. Smith:

*We are praying for you. We are not expecting
an answer.*

Without realizing it, that little girl summed up the prayer life of many Christians: *We are praying for you. We are not expecting an answer.* The truth is, most of us aren't surprised when our prayers are not answered—we're surprised when they are. The opposite should be true.

171

When I flip a light switch in my house, I'm not surprised when the lights come on. When I turn on the ignition in my car (I know this illustration is iffy), I'm not surprised when the engine roars to life. And I shouldn't be surprised when God answers my prayer. God intended that our prayers be answered. While the Bible admits the fact of unanswered prayer, it never assumes it. Answered prayer should be the rule, not the exception.

Yet prayer is one of the biggest mysteries of the Christian faith. At times, when we've had a succession of answered prayers, we feel that at last we've finally learned how to pray. Then we have long stretches when God seems to have stuffed cotton in His ears and all we get is a busy signal.

No wonder the disciples said to Jesus, "Lord, teach us to pray." Mark it well: Prayer does not come naturally or effortlessly — it must be learned. It is good to know that we have the greatest of all teachers and that His desire to teach far surpasses our desire to learn.

A Pattern Prayer

In learning to pray, two problems must be dealt with: *how* to pray and *what* to pray for. Every problem we encounter in prayer revolves around these two questions — and Jesus answers both in Matthew 6:1-13.

This passage is, of course, part of the Sermon on the Mount. Here Jesus gives His disciples both the spiritual conditions and the specific content of the prayer God always answers.

Christ's purpose was not to give us a form prayer to be ritually recited over and over — that would contradict what He said about "vain repetition" — but to give us an example to follow when we pray. This is a pattern, a blueprint. It covers everything in principle and contains everything that we could ask of God. Every conceivable need we will ever encounter is dealt with in the pattern prayer. When we pray, regardless of the length of our prayer, we are simply expanding the principles found here; we are adding flesh to the skeleton. This is the way to pray, says Jesus. Every prayer built according to these specifications will be answered.

Four ingredients of answered prayer emerge from these verses. But before we examine these four requirements, it will help to view the structure of the passage and see it as a whole. Here is the Master Teacher at work. First, He tells us how NOT to pray, then gives the REASON for not praying that way, and finally, He tells us HOW to pray.

How NOT to Pray

Jesus introduced this section of the Sermon on the Mount with a warning:

> Beware of practicing your righteousness before
> men to be noticed by them; otherwise you have
> no reward with your Father who is in heaven.
> When therefore you give alms, do not sound a
> trumpet before you, as the hypocrites do in the
> synagogues and in the streets, that they may be
> honored by men. Truly I say to you, they have
> their reward in full. But when you give alms, do
> not let your left hand know what your right
> hand is doing that your alms may be in secret;
> and your Father who sees in secret will repay
> you (Matthew 6:1-4).

Jesus warns us of the two most common dangers in prayer—praying like a hypocrite and praying like a heathen:

- The hypocrite prays with the wrong motive.
  The heathen prays in the wrong manner.

- The hypocrite perverts the purpose of prayer.
  The heathen misunderstands the nature of prayer.

- The hypocrite prays to impress man.
  The heathen prays to impress God.

- The hypocrite's mistake is made deliberately.
  The heathen's mistake is made ignorantly.

Don't Pray Like the Hypocrites (verses 5,6)

Something of the hypocrite and the heathen hides in all of us. There is the temptation to use prayer to impress others and call attention to ourselves—that's the hypocrite in us. Also, we tend to rush into prayer without thought or preparation, thinking God will be persuaded by long and loud praying—that's the heathen in us. These two errors choke the life from true prayer and must be avoided. Jesus tells us how in these verses.

The **negative** teaching:

And when you pray, you are not to be as the hypocrites; for they love to stand and pray in the synagogues and on street corners, in order to be SEEN BY MEN (verse 5a).

The **reason**:

Truly I say to you, they HAVE THEIR REWARD in full (5b).

The **positive** teaching:

But you, when you pray, go into your inner
room, and when you have shut your door, PRAY
to your Father who is IN SECRET, and your
Father who sees in secret will repay you
(verse 6).

Don't Pray Like the Heathen (verses 7-13)

The **negative** teaching:

And when you are praying, DO NOT USE MEAN-
INGLESS REPETITION, as the Gentiles do, for
they suppose that they will be heard for their
many words (verse 7).

The **reason**:

Therefore do not be like them; for YOUR FATHER
KNOWS WHAT YOU NEED, before you ask Him
(verse 8).

The **positive** teaching:

Pray, then, in this way:
"Our Father who art in heaven,
Hallowed be Thy name.
Thy kingdom come.
Thy will be done,
On earth as it is in heaven.
Give us this day our daily bread.
And forgive us our debts, as we also have
forgiven our debtors.
And do not lead us into temptation, but
deliver us from evil. (For Thine is the
kingdom, and the power, and the glory,
forever. Amen)" (verses 9-13, NASB).

How TO Pray

Now let's turn our attention to the four ingredients of the prayer God always answers.

1. We Must Pray With Sincerity (verse 5)

Prayer's first demand is sincerity, evidenced in verse 5. Jesus is not condemning public praying, but praying "to be seen by men."

Here is a sobering truth. The highest and holiest act of man is prayer; surely in the inner sanctum of the prayer closet we are safe from sin. Even here, though, we cannot escape sin's penetrating and perverting power. Our holiest moments can become the occasion for the greatest of sins. Impure thoughts, unworthy motives intrude into the most sacred place and wipe their muddy feet arrogantly on the floor of the throne room.

Our loftiest acts are sometimes inspired by the lowest of motives. "Vanity," said Napoleon, "was the cause of the revolution. Liberty was only a pretext." It may be that in the attempt to pray we discover the truth about ourselves; perhaps in the hidden altar of prayer we meet the ultimate test of our "interior" purity.

Our praying becomes hypocrisy when we make it a spiritual status symbol. We play the hypocrite when we use prayer to impress others. Public prayer, especially, is susceptible to this temptation.

Not long ago I was speaking at a conference where the chairman was noted for his eloquent public prayers. People constantly praised the beauty of his prayers—in his presence. It was too much for any mortal to bear. When he stood to pray (which he did more and more frequently), he affected an unnatural, sonorous pulpit voice and piled up mountains of ostentatious phrases. Shakespeare would have been impressed. For this man, prayer had become a performance, a public exhibition. When we use prayer to draw attention to ourselves, we are in fact praying to men rather than to God, seeking their applause rather than His blessing.

This perversion of prayer can be subtle. I was away in a meeting, a thousand miles from home, eating breakfast in the hotel restaurant. When the waitress brought my plate I bowed my head and thanked God for it. Half an egg later a couple appeared at my table and asked if I was Ronald Dunn. I confessed that I was.

"When you came into the restaurant," the man said, "I told my wife it was you but we weren't certain."

Then his wife said, "I told my husband we would know it was you if you said grace over your food. We watched you, and when you bowed your head we knew."

Now when I eat alone in a restaurant I don't know if I'm praying over my food because I'm truly thankful or because someone may be watching me. When your spiritual reputation is at stake, a low motive is better than none at all.

Even our private prayer can be afflicted with this malady. Of all our spiritual activities none is as vulnerable to vain display. I think most Christians have an inferiority complex where their prayer life is concerned, and hold in awe those who have "learned the secret" of praying. And that makes it tempting to bid for respect by calling attention to the long hours we spend in prayer. In other words, it would be mighty hard to spend the entire night in prayer and not tell someone about it.

At no time must we be more completely sincere and totally honest than when we approach God in prayer. He welcomes us at His throne of grace when we come openly and honestly, without pretense or sham — that is, when we come with a pure motive.

Ah, and there's the rub. Nothing is as difficult to subdue as an impure motive. We are our own worst enemy. Christ's command seems so impossible that we may be discouraged from praying at all. How can we achieve this degree of sincerity in prayer?

The answer lies in the next ingredient of answered prayer.

2. We Must Pray With Secrecy (verse 6)

I once heard it said that the secret of religion is religion in secret. To guard against praying to be seen of men, Jesus tells us to pray where only God can see us—in secret. By this Jesus does not mean that we are never to pray in public; the secrecy of which He speaks is more than physical, although physical secrecy is important and was practiced by our Lord.

As a matter of fact, our public praying should be backed up by our private praying. If we only pray in public, we are hypocrites. Without a faithful, private prayer life, our public prayers are nothing but show.

The secret praying that Jesus speaks of can be done in public. Primarily, it is a mental and spiritual secrecy. The key is the phrase, "Pray to your Father." In public prayer we may pray to the listeners instead of God. I have been in prayer meetings where each person takes his turn praying aloud; where each prayer elicits hearty "amens" with every phrase—until it's my turn. Have you ever noticed how quiet it suddenly gets when it's your turn to pray? And have you ever found yourself ransacking your prayer bin for one that will wring "amens" from your fellow pray-ers?

Or have you perhaps used the family prayer time to preach to your family instead of praying to the

Father? You know, something like this: "Dear Lord, please help Johnnie to see that I can't take him to the zoo tomorrow, and help Sally pick up her dirty clothes and clean her room, and help Bill trim the lawn tomorrow because we're having guests over the weekend."

Secret praying is "praying to the Father." This means that we *concentrate on His presence.* Our attention is focused on Him, His will, His glory. We are more conscious of His presence than we are of the presence of others. Having shut out the world we have shut ourselves in with Him. I have heard a few people who, even in a crowded room, prayed as though there was no one else in the universe but God and them.

Another thing secret praying means is that we are *content with His praise.* Jesus, referring to praying hypocrites, says, "They have their reward" (verse 2). As in the passage on fasting, here He also uses a word that means "payment in full, immediate payment, nothing more to come." Of course, that's what the hypocrite is after—immediate reward. If he wants the praise of men, he can have it. I think that's true of anyone: If a person sets his heart on winning the praise and approval of his contemporaries, if that is his ambition and the driving force of his life, he will probably get exactly what he wants. Anyone who wants it that badly deserves exactly what he gets—but that is all he gets. "They have their reward," in full and final payment.

When Jesus refers to the reward from the Father, He uses a different word as He did on the subject of fasting—a word that indicates a recompense to be paid, like interest accruing on an investment. We have a reward now in answered prayers, in the peace of God that comes through communion with Him, in seeing

God work in answer to our requests, in the deepening of our fellowship with Him, and in a hundred more ways. We have even more and greater rewards coming to us when we stand in His presence and receive the gifts of His praise. Nothing will satisfy the hypocrite but the praise of man; nothing will satisfy the "secret pray-er" but the praise of God.

Imagine that you are an actor or actress performing in a stage play. You are the performer on stage; the audience is seated before you. When the play is done, you listen for the applause from the audience. When you have played to the audience, and they in turn have applauded you, you have your reward.

When you pray before a congregation, you must remember that the congregation is not an audience. You do not "play" to them. *God is the audience,* and you "play" to Him, seeking His applause, His praise, His approval.

This kind of person will have no trouble praying sincerely in public or in private.

3. We Must Pray With Simplicity (verses 7,8)

It is not repetition that Jesus condemns here, but *meaningless* repetition. The Greek word is difficult to translate into English but it carries the idea of babbling or rambling on and on in a torrent of words. "And when you pray, do not keep on babbling like pagans," is the New International Version's rendering.

The heathen believed their gods were impressed with the amount of time spent and the number of words uttered in prayer. To them prayer was primarily a matter of convincing their gods that they were worthy of the blessing they were seeking. It was prayer by attrition, wearing the god down until he would give what was asked.

It's amazing how pagan we can be in praying. Listen to yourself the next time you pray; you may find that much of your praying is trying to talk God into seeing things your way. I admit that much of my own praying has been, at times, nothing more than an attempt to get God to believe in me, or to cooperate with me in some venture of my own making, as though I were prying open the hand of a tight-fisted God.

Don't pray like that, Jesus tells us. Why not? "For your Father knows what you need, before you ask Him" (verse 8). The heathen prayed incorrectly because their notion of God was incorrect.

It is God's character that determines how we pray; therefore, in prayer, the chief thing is knowing what kind of God we are praying to. Augustine prayed, "Grant me, Lord, to know which is first, to call on Thee or to praise Thee. And again, to know Thee or to call on Thee. *For who can call on Thee, not knowing Thee? For he that knoweth Thee not may call on Thee as other than Thou art*" (emphasis added).

"Your Father," is how Jesus described God; and He told us to say, "Our Father," when we pray (verse 9). This is the first time these words are addressed to God in the Bible. The notion is unique to the New Testament, but sadly, the concept seems lost to a great part of contemporary Christianity. When Jesus prayed, He said, "Father." (The one exception was when Jesus was on the cross and cried, "My God, my God, why hast Thou forsaken me?") Paul's prayers were addressed to "the God and Father of our Lord Jesus Christ." We are instructed to pray with the simplicity of a child speaking to his father and with the surety of a child whose father already knows his every need.

Some believe that the statement that God already knows what we need implies we need not ask. If God already knows, why bother? If He knows we need it and He wants us to have it, we'll get it. One popular Bible teacher said all this business of retreating to a prayer closet and petitioning God for things is nothing but "religious gymnastics." The only thing wrong with that is, it's wrong.

It is obvious Jesus did not intend us to interpret Him in that way. In the verses that follow the model prayer, He tells us to pray specifically for certain things, and one of those petitions is for daily bread. The Father surely knows we need that before we ask.

These words are meant to *encourage*, not discourage, us to pray. We are to pray with the confidence generated by the realization that we don't have to convince God of what we need; He was convinced before we even learned of the need.

When my son was in college, most weekends he would make the hour-and-a-half drive home in a huge, black, senile Thunderbird that I had passed down to him, to which he had added glass-packs and an "a-oo-gaa" horn, and which he had named Murphy, after "Murphy's Law" (if anything can go wrong, it will). When he was home I would usually inspect the beast to see if it needed any repairs.

One Saturday morning he meandered nonchalantly into my study, absently looking around, and eased into a conversation about his car. He started slowly and calmly and rapidly progressed to fast and intense. He was trying to convince me that his car needed new tires, that he didn't have the money, that the need was so urgent maybe I could loan him the money, and so on — talk about meaningless repetition. When he stopped to catch his breath I jumped in and said, "Steve, I looked at your car this morning — I know you need new tires."

"You do?"

"I do."

His whole approach changed when he learned he didn't have to convince me of his need. "Prayer," said Richard Trench, "is not overcoming God's reluctance; it is laying hold to God's willingness."

Repetition in prayer is not always meaningless. In the two parables Jesus gave us on prayer (Luke 11:4-9 and 18:1-8), the emphasis is on persistent repetition. Jesus repeated Himself three times when He prayed in Gethsemane. Repetition can be the sighs of a burdened heart, a burden so intense we can't help but cry out repeatedly to God.

4. We Should Pray Specifically (verse 9)

How is this simplicity accomplished? Jesus tells us in the next verse: "Pray, then, in this way" (verse 9). Having told us the wrong way to pray, He now shows us the right way. Simple praying is specific praying. The specifics are laid down in the Model Prayer.

As I mentioned earlier, Jesus intended the prayer to be more than a formal benediction. It is good and right that we should use it in our worship, both in private and in public, but that is not its paramount purpose. It is first and foremost a pattern to guide us in our praying.

Two facts deserve notice: **One**, prayer is an *act*. While we should live in an attitude of prayer, prayer is more than an attitude. It is not merely, as one put it, living in the awareness that all things are ours in Christ. For Christ, prayer was an act with a beginning and an ending: "When Jesus *ceased* praying" (Luke 11:1, emphasis added); "When you *pray, say*" (Luke 11:2, emphasis added).

Two, prayer is *asking*. Prayer is petition, not praise. Our private worship should, of course, include praise, and during times of prayer we should praise God, but prayer and praise are not the same thing. Of the various biblical words used to denote prayer, the vast majority are, almost without exception, unashamedly words of petition.

I labor this point because the church seems to have rediscovered praise — and there is tremendous emphasis on it in both teaching and singing. However, the momentum created by this emphasis has caused some to overshoot the point of balance.

Not long ago a fellow conference speaker, in a message on praise, stated that as we mature in Christ, praise will replace petition — there will be less asking and more praising. He went so far as to suggest that if we are still at the "petition level" of prayer, we are carnal. I could hardly resist the urge to leap up and say, "If that is so, then Jesus was carnal," because His prayers were almost totally prayers of petition — petitions for Himself. The prayers of Paul were petitionary. Both Christ and Paul admonished us to ask and keep on asking.

The Model Prayer is 100 percent petition. Even the phrase, "Hallowed be Thy name," is petition. Jesus was not saying, "When you pray, the first thing you should do is hallow the name of the Father." He said, "When you pray, say, 'Thy name be hallowed.' " That is a petition, asking that God's name will be hallowed and revered.

The Model Prayer is made up of six petitions, imperatives in the form of commands. In each instance we are asking God to do something specific. The prayer is in two parts, with three petitions in each part. A proper exposition of the prayer demands a volume of its own; here we can only mention the main points.

The first part of the prayer concerns *the glory of the Father* (verses 9,10).

The prayer God always answers gives priority to the glory of the Father, putting His interests before our own. This implies an emptying of self and an occupation with the things of God. Only after we have thus forgotten ourselves can we think of ourselves.

1. We are to pray that the name of God will be revered: "Hallowed be Thy name."

2. We are to pray that the rule of God will be established: "Thy kingdom come."

3. We are to pray that the will of God be done: "Thy will be done."

The second part of the prayer concerns *the good of the Family,* physically and spiritually.

1. We are to pray for daily provision: "Give us this day our daily bread."

2. We are to pray for daily pardon: "Forgive us our debts."

3. We are to pray for daily protection: "Do not lead us into temptation, but deliver us from evil."

At the beginning of the Model Prayer is a phrase that casts its shadow over the entire prayer, setting the stage for its petitions and forming the foundation of all true prayer: "Our Father." These two words sum up the whole prayer.

Our. It is so obvious that we often miss it. *Our* Father. *Our* daily bread. *Our* debts. Lead *us*. Deliver *us*. This is *family* prayer. No child of God ever prays alone. In a sense, when one child prays, the entire family prays. Here is a hint of what Jesus would mean later when He would pray for His followers, "that they may all be one; even as Thou, Father, art in Me, and I in Thee" (John 17:21).

Our. This is intercession—unselfish intercession. The family member prays, not only for himself, but for every member of the family. What he seeks for himself, he seeks for the whole family. As a member of the family of God, as a constituent of its oneness, I have no right to ask something for myself that I wouldn't want every member to have. Whatever prayer finally is, it is not a means whereby I can forge ahead of others, possess more than others, occupy a more favored position with the Father, enable my church to grow larger and wealthier than the church across the street.

Father is the other word. Here is the requirement of all prayer. Prayer is a family matter and only those who can say "Our Father" can truly pray.

Here is our right to pray. We are not beggars cowering at the back door pleading for a handout. We are children seated at the Father's table. J. D. Jones tells the story of a Roman emperor who was entering Rome in triumph after a victorious battle. As the magnificent procession moved down the street, a small child suddenly darted through the fence of soldiers lining the street and headed for the opulent carriage that bore the emperor. One of the soldiers grabbed him, saying, "That is the emperor!"

The child broke loose and, racing for the carriage, cried back, "*Your* emperor, *my* father!"

What right have we to imagine God would suffer the likes of us in His throne room, and listen to our pitiful requests?

When we pray, we are to say, *"Our Father."*

A Silence in Heaven

God did not answer the two biggest prayers of my life. I wanted those more than all the other answers put together, and I would gladly have forfeited them all for those two. I was surprised, bewildered and hurt.

I was surprised because I knew God would answer them. He had given Kaye and me a promise; we had a "word" from God, and we had done everything we were supposed to do: We believed, prayed in faith, confessed, claimed, pleaded the blood, rebuked the devil, thanked God in advance for the answers—we even fasted. God had answered plenty of prayers like that before.

I was bewildered because I was writing a book on prayer; I was traveling the country telling people how to pray and helping churches establish prayer ministries. My own church's flourishing prayer ministry was attracting attention from distant places. I knew how to pray. Prayer was my specialty.

I was hurt (angry?) because God had betrayed me. Like Jeremiah, I wanted to say, "O Lord, You enticed me, and I was persuaded" (Jeremiah 20:7). He had strung me along, tantalizing me with big answers to small prayers, but when the Big One came along, nothing. No answer, no explanation, nothing. Heaven was silent.

My prayer life shriveled. When I tried to pray, those two unanswered prayers hovered over me like two grinning demons, clacking: "What's this? Are you praying *again*? It didn't do much good last time, did it? You're wasting your time."

The prayers died in my throat.

I think I felt like C. S. Lewis must have felt when he wrote:

> Meanwhile, where is God? This is one of the most disquieting symptoms. When you are happy, so happy that you have no sense of needing Him, if you turn to Him with praise, you will be welcomed with open arms. But go to Him when your need is desperate, when all other help is vain and what do you find? A door slammed in your face, and a sound of bolting and double bolting on the inside. After that, silence. You may as well turn away.[1]

But God didn't let it end like that in my life. He pursued the rebel, loving him, tutoring him, until he understood that he would never understand. I learned that my feelings were a result of ignorance on my part, not indifference on His. God is bigger than our theology; our concept of prayer does not bind Him. God makes no terms and gives no promises that paralyze His sovereignty. Interpretation or application of Scripture that does not leave God's sovereignty intact is a wrong interpretation. My expectations do not bind Him. My wish is not His command.

The Ground Rules

The other evening I sat with a mother and father who just a couple of months before had buried their teenage son. As a child he had been struck by a crippling disease. Death was inevitable. We talked about things survivors always talk about. We phrased and rephrased our questions, but regardless of their shape they all amounted to the same question: Why? It's hard not to ask that question standing at the window watching the neighbors' kids running and yelling and laughing. A little light from the Lord would go a long way. That's not too much to ask, is it?

After deliberating for two hours we still came up short. I said the only thing I knew to say. When all is said and done it comes down to this: "God is in heaven and you are on earth" (Ecclesiastes 5:2).

It's good to keep that in mind. Those are the ground rules.

> Between God and man there is a hollow space which man is unable of himself to penetrate. If it were possible for him to do this, he would have power over his relationship with God, and thus have power over God Himself. But no creature has such power. The contention that the creature possesses this power is idol-worship.[2]

We don't accept that "hollow space," though. Mystery is intolerable simply because it reminds us of our helplessness. This is why Jacob, having realized that the "man" he was wrestling was an angel with divine powers, asked, "Tell me Your name, I pray" (Genesis 32:29).

Ancient man believed himself to be surrounded by divine powers which determined his destiny, and if he ever found himself in the visible, tangible presence of one, the thing to do was hang on to it, not to let it go, to bind it to himself so its divine power could be used to his own ends. The belief was that if you knew its name you could summon it, you could obligate it, you could even arbitrarily manipulate it.

> Thus, embedded in this most urgent of all human questions, this question about the name, is all man's need, all his boldness before God. . . . There is no need which can smother this ancient human thirst to find God and to bind Him to oneself.[3]

A similar incident is found in Judges when Manoah encounters the angel of God that appeared to his wife with the promise of Samson's birth. Manoah asks the same question Jacob asked, "What is Your name, that when Your words come to pass we may honor You?" (Judges 13:17) But his name is hidden (verse 18), too awesome and sacred to be spoken, and like Jacob's mysterious intruder, the angel does not answer the question. He does not permit his mystery and freedom to be touched.

God's Mysterious Freedom

God remains free to act as He chooses. Take, for example, the Scripture that is the text for this book: Ezekiel 22:30: "So I sought for a man among them who would make up a wall, and stand in the gap before me on behalf of the land, that I should not destroy it; but I found no one." The result? "Therefore I have poured out my indignation on them" (verse 31). Because there was no intercessor, God poured out His wrath.

Then in Isaiah 59:16 we read: "He saw that there was no man, and wondered that there was no intercessor." Again, God looks for an intercessor, a man to stand in the gap, but He finds none. The result? "Therefore His own arm brought salvation for Him; and His own righteousness, it sustained Him." Because there was no intercessor, God brought forth His salvation.

In Ezekiel, finding no man gave God the opportunity to display His power in judgment. In Isaiah, finding no man gave God the opportunity to display His power in salvation.

If we believe that all roses are red and someone brings us a yellow rose, we will say it is a fake — all roses are red. And here is where we get into trouble; we have a bad habit of anticipating God, of forming a mental image of God answering our prayer, with time, place and method included.

We can see it; it's obvious there's only one way our prayer can be answered, only one way the problem can be solved. Anybody can see that.

I can't recall many times when God worked exactly as I expected. He has a way of taking the obvious and reversing it. Sometimes the answer is so unlike our picture that we think God has not answered at all. The Jewish nation did something like that with Jesus. He did not look like they thought the Messiah should look, so they concluded He was not the Messiah.

To this hour the ways of God answering prayer remain a mystery to me. Which is as it should be — who would want to worship a God he could understand?

Slow to Believe

I find myself in excellent company. Some mighty good people carry in their heart divine surprises: surprise answers and surprise non-answers. Two who helped me a lot are Zacharias and Elizabeth, the parents of John the Baptist.

Luke introduces us to this couple in the first chapter of his Gospel as a "certain priest named Zacharias" and his wife Elizabeth, both of whom were righteous and blameless in the sight of God. "But they had no child, because Elizabeth was barren, and they were both well advanced in years" (Luke 1:5-7).

One day while Zacharias was burning incense in the temple, an angel appeared on the right side of the altar of incense and said, "Do not be afraid, Zacharias, for your prayer is heard; and your wife Elizabeth will bear you a son, and you shall call his name John" (verses 11-13).

Then Zacharias asked a phenomenal question: "How shall I know this? For I am an old man, and my wife is well advanced in years" (verse 18). I call that a phenomenal question because if an angel suddenly appeared before me and told me my prayer was answered, I would tend to believe him. And this particular angel was no mail-room clerk — this was Gabriel, "who stands in the presence of God" (verse 19). Yet even the personal appearance of an angel with a special delivery message did not convince Zacharias. So God struck Zacharias dumb because he did not believe the angel's words. If

God dealt with unbelief that way today, most of us would spend the rest of our lives speechless.

Zacharias had a good reason for asking his question: Years of unanswered prayer had made him slow to believe. This prayer Gabriel was referring to, their prayer for a child, must have been close to prehistoric, for they were both well past the age of childbearing. By the way, doesn't Zacharias phrase it beautifully? "How shall I know this? For I am an old man, *and my wife is well advanced in years.*" He didn't say, "I'm an old man and my wife is an old woman." The old King James says it best: "My wife is *well-stricken* in years." Zacharias was a delicate diplomat.

We must not be too hard on him for doubting the angel's words. His dreams of being a father had long since surrendered to reality. And yet . . .

. . . here was an angel straight from God, avowing it was going to happen. Zacharias began to learn some things about how God answers prayer. As we follow his story in the next chapter, perhaps we, too, can learn.

P.S. We see into the past a lot better than we see in the present, and now, reflecting back on those two unanswered prayers, I think I learned more about prayer and more about God from those than from all the answered ones combined. Who knows, by the time I get to heaven I may even think God did the right thing.

How God Answers Prayer

Zacharias was surprised when God answered his prayer.

I was surprised when God didn't answer mine.

I liked Zacharias's surprise better than mine. Since he had better success with his prayer we'd better let him show us how God answers prayer.

God Answers Later

When does God answer prayer?

He always answers immediately but sometimes later.

I'm not trying to be clever. When we offer an "answerable" prayer, that is, one that is according to His will (1 John 5:14,15), He hears and answers immediately. The Lord doesn't convene a committee to examine the facts and advise and consent. Nor does He need time to consider the request. "And it shall come to pass, that before they call, I will answer, and while they are yet speaking, I will hear" (Isaiah 65:24).

The *granting* of the prayer is immediate, but the *giving* of it into our hands may be delayed.

This is what the angel was trying to tell Zacharias: "Your prayer is heard" (Luke 1:13). The wording makes it appear that Zacharias had been praying for a son even as he ministered in the temple that day. The fact is, Zacharias and Elizabeth's prayer for a son was no longer current. Zacharias's question to the angel shows that they had long since given up on it. Their desire for a child was a discarded hope. Now we can better understand his question.*

There is another clue to the answer to this previously abandoned prayer of Zacharias and Elizabeth. The phrase, "Your prayer is heard," is important. The tense of the Greek word translated "heard" can be expressed, "was heard," and in keeping with the context, it should be. This was a prayer that had been offered in the past — and answered in the past.

In the Greek text, "heard" has a prefix attached to it, making it a rare word, occurring only five times in the New Testament. The prefix expresses purpose, action, tendency, result. With the prefix and the verb joined, a literal translation is, "Your prayer was *heard-*

---

* Author's note: Some interpreters hold that Zacharias's prayer would have to be in keeping with his presence at the altar. A prayer for personal blessing would be unthinkable and unworthy of his position, so his prayer for a son was actually a prayer for the salvation of the people or for the promised Messiah. This strained interpretation, though, ignores the context and the personal pronouns, e.g., "*your* wife shall bear *you* a son."

to-do." When God heard their prayer, He also *did* it. God had granted their request years before, perhaps, and now He was going to *give* it.

We see this same idea in the tenth chapter of Daniel. The prophet had prayed and fasted for three weeks without receiving an answer of any kind. Then an angel appeared with this message:

> Do not fear, Daniel, for from the *first day* that you set your heart to understand, and to humble yourself before your God, your words were heard; and I have come because of your words. But the prince of the kingdom of Persia withstood me twenty-one days; and behold, Michael, one of the chief princes, came to help me, for I had been left alone there with the kings of Persia (Daniel 10:12,13, NKJ, emphasis added).

This isn't the place to clear all the cobwebs out of those words—what is significant for our purpose is the fact that Daniel prayed and fasted for three weeks, and at the end of that time an angel arrived with an answer and an explanation. Daniel's prayers had been heard the first day he had uttered them, and on that first day the angel had been dispatched with an answer, but he had been held up by heavy traffic for twenty-one days.

"From the first day . . . your words were heard." The *granting* was immediate but the *giving* was delayed.

We are all familiar with this prayer promise: "Therefore I say to you, whatever things you ask when you pray, believe that you receive them, and you will have them" (Mark 11:24). The New English Bible reads, "I tell you, then, whatever you ask for in prayer, believe that you *have received it* and *it will be yours*" (emphasis added).

The Williams translation highlights the sense of the Greek tenses: "So then I tell you, whenever you pray and ask for anything, have faith that it *has been granted* you, and you *will get it*" (emphasis added).

It doesn't take much faith to believe you have something when you already have it. To believe you have something when you don't yet have it—that's faith.

God Answers Better

Zacharias also learned that God often answers later in order to answer better.

On my desk is a pencil holder with this motto: "God always gives the best to those who leave the choice with Him." Is that true?

I think some people believe the Bible because they don't know what it says. For example, the Bible says in Psalm 34:10 that "those who seek the LORD shall not lack any good thing." In Psalm 84:11 it makes this promise: "No good thing will He withhold from those who walk uprightly." Do we really believe that?

Then why do we complain when He withholds something from us? If it had been a good thing for us, He would have given it to us. Ruth Graham, the wife of Billy Graham, is quoted as saying, "If God answered every prayer of mine, I would have married the wrong man seven times." Thank God for some unanswered prayers.

God not only answers later, but He also answers better. Suppose God had given Zacharias and Elizabeth a son when they first asked for one, in their young years. To be sure, they would have been thrilled and they would have loved him with all their hearts. But in the final analysis, he would have been just another boy who had been born, lived his life and died, a handful of unremembered dust. No one would remember him today; no sermons would be preached about him; his name, and the names of his parents, would not have been immortalized in the Scriptures.

God gave them something better. He gave them John the Baptist, the last Old Testament prophet, the only Old Testament prophet who lived to see his prophecy fulfilled. He was the first cousin of Jesus Christ, the forerunner of the Messiah, the man of whom Jesus said of "those born of women, there has not risen one greater" than he (Matthew 11:11).

God gave Zacharias and Elizabeth the unexpected joy of a son in their old age, a joy rarely experienced by couples their age, a joy multiplied by the long years of waiting. As their years declined, their joy soared. God saved the best till last.

There's a good chance, of course, that at the time, Zacharias and Elizabeth would not have agreed. Probably, they didn't think it was better to wait until they were old. *But we know better.*

God Answers When the Situation Becomes Humanly Impossible

Zacharias discovered that God often waits until the situation is humanly impossible.

A strange thing happened shortly after our church started its intercessory prayer ministry. One Sunday morning at the conclusion of the worship service, a young woman with a pained look on her face drew me aside and began whispering to me. She was one of several women in our church who had enlisted in the new prayer ministry with high hopes for their unsaved husbands. That had been three months ago.

"There's something wrong," she whispered.

"What is it?"

"My husband," she said. "I've been praying for him for three months and . . . "

"And?"

Tears came to her eyes and she was trying hard not to cry. "He's worse than ever," she blurted out. "He's more hostile toward God, toward the church, toward me. It's not getting better — it's getting worse."

I had received similar reports from others. A man had come to my study several months back and we had covenanted together to pray about a serious financial problem in his business. Later, when I asked him how things were going, he shook his head and admitted, "Terrible." Putting his hand on my shoulder, he said jokingly (I think), "You know, preacher, sometimes I wish you had never got me into this praying business."

This is one of God's ways: He often allows a situation to deteriorate before He intervenes. With Zacharias and Elizabeth He waited until both were well past the age of childbearing. When it was physically impossible, God gave them a son.

Sometimes things do get worse before they get better. I caution would-be intercessors not to be surprised if this occurs. I have watched people for whom I was praying gradually shift from indifference to hostility. That, I believe, may be a symptom of the Spirit's convicting activity. When God closes in on an individual, that person cannot remain indifferent — and you can expect the enemy to mount a counter-attack to recapture lost ground.

In other words, I have discovered that whatever I am praying about, *on its way to better, it may drop by worse for a visit.*

God worked this way with Abraham and Sarah. He promised Abraham he would be a father of many nations, that all nations of the earth would be blessed through his seed, a seed so vast it would be easier to count the number of stars in heaven than to number the issue of his seed. And Abraham "believed in the LORD" (Genesis 15:6).

It's hard to keep believing when old age overtakes you and nothing has happened. So hard to believe, in fact, that you run in a replacement, like Abraham ran in Ishmael. God waited until Abraham was 100 years old and Sarah was 90 before He *gave* what He had already *granted*.

Even when God freshened the promise (Genesis 17), Abraham found it hard to believe. He . . .

> laughed, and said in his heart, "Shall a child be born to a man who is one hundred years old? And shall Sarah, who is ninety years old, bear a child?" (Genesis 17:17)

Abraham laughed. He couldn't help himself — the idea was ridiculous. He laughed because he didn't believe.

We know Sarah didn't believe it either, because she also laughed. If a 90-year-old woman discovers she's pregnant, there are any number of things she might do — but laughing is not one of them.

Why does God work in this way?

God Answers for His Glory

God always takes the route that brings Him the greatest glory. I believe we can file that under Heaven's Fixed Laws. As we saw in chapter 4, the motive behind our asking and the motive behind His answering is "that the Father may be glorified in the Son" (John 14:13). The further back we track these things, the more we will see that everything leads to this destination: the glory of God. Abraham was "strengthened in faith, giving glory to God" (Romans 4:20). When bearing children was no longer possible, when Abraham could no longer take matters into his own hands as he had done in the case of Ishmael, God moved. And when finally the child was born, there was no doubt that God had done it—He received the credit and the glory.

Because we don't understand this, God seems at times to stand idly by while we sink beneath the waves. Hurt and outraged by His apathy, we cry, "Master, carest Thou not that we perish?" But that is *our* opinion. We are not perishing, and He is not unconcerned.

I remember the first time I heard Manley Beasley speak. It was an informal gathering, not more than fifty or sixty people, ministers and their wives, mostly. Manley, an evangelist and revivalist, was surfacing from a two-year bout with five diseases, three of which were terminal (at least, they were supposed to be). Only days out of the hospital and too weak to stand, he sat on a high stool and, in obvious pain, spoke in a soft voice. His opening words were: "Folks, God won't hurt you."

At the time, God was killing me.

That was my opinion. God was not killing me; He was saving me (I remembered reading something about losing your life to save it). Like Moses, I wanted to see the face of God; I wanted to see Him from the front; I wanted a glance at the script. Before I followed Him I wanted to know where He was going.

Yet, like Moses, I travel under sealed orders. I see God only in retrospect. When I pause and look back at the way I've come, I see the hand of God at every turn and know that the Savior has led each step of the way.

This fact, perhaps more than any other, has cushioned me in rough times when answers were long in coming. It has become a buffer that keeps the sharp edges of living from severing the jugular.

Remember: *God takes the route that brings Him the most glory.*

And: *On its way to better, it may drop by worse.*

God Answers According to Divine Necessity

Zacharias also learned that God answers prayer when it is linked to divine necessity.

I know God has no "needs" and no "problems," but I want to use these words to illustrate this point. Why did God choose that particular time to answer Zacharias's prayer? Why not ten years earlier? Why not ten years later? I believe God answered when He did because He "needed" to answer then. The fullness of time had come, and He "needed" John the Baptist. God "needed" the forerunner of the Messiah, and in meeting Zacharias's need, He met His own. By solving Zacharias's problem, He solved His own.

And then there is Hannah. Her story is told in the first chapter of 1 Samuel. In her struggle with the stigma of barrenness, she personifies the reproach endured by all the childless women of the Bible. Year after year Hannah cried before the Lord, begging Him to remove her disgrace and give her a son. Her burden was so great she could not express it in words; she groaned her supplication to God, moving her lips but uttering no sound. When Eli, the priest, saw her in the temple praying with such emotion, he accused her of being drunk.

The Lord answered her prayer — finally. He gave her a son, Samuel, whom she gave back to the Lord, and who became the great judge and prophet of Israel.

When did God answer her prayer? When He "needed" to. There came a time when God "needed" Samuel, when Israel "needed" a judge and a prophet, and in solving Hannah's "problem," He solved His own.

God always moves with redemptive purpose. Jesus performed many miracles — but not a one for show. I remember when I was a boy sitting in the balcony of the old Temple Theater, seeing for the first time the original (and silent) black-and-white classic, *The King of Kings*. I watched the soldiers drag Jesus before Herod. When Herod demanded that Jesus work a miracle, I leaned forward in my seat to urge Jesus on — if Herod saw a miracle, he would let Jesus go. I knew how the story ended, but I got caught up in the drama. I couldn't believe that Jesus would just stand there and not even speak to Herod; all He had to do was work one little miracle and He would have gone free.

Why didn't He? He could have — and it seemed to me a mighty good time to do one. Besides, weren't the miracles intended as signs of His Messiahship? Why didn't He dazzle old Herod with one?

That kind of miracle had been pre-empted by the redemptive purpose of God. Jesus confined His miracles to that realm. Standing silent before Herod, Jesus knew His hour had come, the hour He spoke of in John 12:27. He did not want to escape from Herod and his soldiers, or from Pilate, or from the Jewish leaders and their mobs, for He had come to die.

God Answers According to His Will

Our prayers must be linked to divine necessity; they must flow in the stream of God's redemptive activity — according to the will of God.

"According to the will of God" is another intimidating phrase in the Christian vocabulary. This, perhaps, more than any other one thing, discourages Christians from praying with confidence. It's scary to think that we might miss God's will and spend the rest of our lives paying for it.

We cannot know the will of God about details of our lives, and we do not need to know the will of God about everything we pray for. That is, the *immediate* will of God. But we can know the *ultimate* will of God. For example, I may be unemployed and unable to provide for my family. I can pray with assurance for my needs to be met because God has promised to supply them (Philippians 4:19). That is what I would call the ultimate will of God. The immediate will of God has to do with *how* God meets that need, the *modus operandi*. I know that when I ask God to meet my needs I am praying according to the will of God. I may not have the same assurance if I ask God to meet my needs by allowing me to win a million dollars from the Publishers' Clearing House Sweepstakes. Winning the million dollars involves the *immediate* will of God. I know God will supply my needs, but He may not do it by making me a millionaire. In fact, I know he won't. I've asked.

What to Say When You Don't Know What to Say

There is a way to know that we are praying according to His will. In His last public discourse, as He drew within sight of the cross, Jesus laid bare His distress:

> Now My soul is troubled, and what shall I say?
> "Father, save me from this hour"? But for this
> purpose I came to this hour. *Father, glorify
> Your name* (John 12:27,28, emphasis added).

"Troubled" in the depth of His being, Jesus debated within Himself: "What shall I say?" He could ask His Father to save Him from the cross. But this "hour" was the reason He came into the world. This is a remarkable drawing aside of the mystery of the God-Man to allow us a glimpse of the humanness of Jesus. "What shall I say?" Would we ever have dreamed that the Son of God would be at a loss for words, so deeply divided within Himself that He would cry, "What shall I say"?

He settled the conflict with these words: "Father, glorify Your name." That's what to say when you don't know what to say. That's what to pray when you don't know what to pray. It is always right to say, "Father, glorify Your name." When we throw that blanket over our petitions, and truly mean it, we are praying in the will of God.

To me, this means that the glory of God, the honor of His name, outranks all petitions; it means that if I must choose (assuming I had the right to choose) between God being glorified and my petition being answered, I would choose the glory of God.

One Friday afternoon when I was in college, a friend and I decided to drive home for the weekend. We piled into my '46 Ford and, both of us being ministerial students, I asked my friend to pray for a safe trip. I bowed my head, closed my eyes and heard him say, "Dear Lord, we pray that You will protect us and grant us traveling mercies — unless we can glorify Thee better on a hospital bed."

That was the last time I asked him to pray about anything. Still, in a crazy kind of way, my friend was right. Whatever we pray for, it is a given that the glory of God takes precedence. Sometimes God withholds the lesser in order to give the greater, and it may be that He cannot give me what I ask without compromising His own plan. So we must pray as Jesus prayed: "Father, if it is Your will, remove this cup from Me; nevertheless, not My will, but Yours, be done" (Luke 22:42).

How Long?

I'm often asked, "How long should we pray for something?" If God delays the answer as He did with Zacharias, how can we know if it's a delay or a denial? We don't want to keep asking for something God has said no to. On the other hand, we don't want to give up if He is telling us to wait.

I suggest that we pray and keep on praying until one of three things occurs:

1. **Until we receive the answer.** Some say it is a lack of faith to ask more than once for the same thing, an act of unbelief that voids our prayer. The argument runs something like this: At four o'clock a boy asks his father to take him to the ball park the next day; the father says yes, he will. At five o'clock the boy asks again, and the father again says that he will. At six

o'clock the boy asks again, and again at seven o'clock, and again at eight. Why does the boy keep asking? Obviously, he doesn't believe his father. And this certainly grieves the father. Thus, if we really have faith, we need ask only once.

I admit this sounds reasonable (and it may have some merit) but I don't think it's scriptural. Jesus believed in persistence. He gave us only two parables about prayer, and the emphasis in both is on persistence (the friend at midnight, Luke 11, and the woman and the judge, Luke 18). In Matthew 7:7-11 Jesus tells us to ask, to seek, and to knock. The tenses of the verbs say ask and keep on asking, seek and keep on seeking, knock and keep on knocking. So we need to ask and keep on asking until we receive, or . . .

2. Until we have the assurance that we will receive it. In the early days of our church prayer ministry, a group of women met each week to pray. It happened that they all went to the same hairdresser, who was not a Christian. They prayed for her for weeks and weeks, until one day when they came together to pray, they couldn't pray for the girl's salvation. Instead, they found themselves thanking God for her salvation; a peace had settled in their hearts about the whole matter. Later, one of the women said she actually felt guilty because she had lost her burden for the girl and no longer prayed for her salvation. About three weeks later, in the Sunday morning service, the hairdresser came to Christ. Everybody was surprised except the women who had prayed for her.

Sometimes when we are praying for something, there will come a quiet assurance that God has heard and answered. Where there was a burden, now there is peace.

3. Until God says no. By spiritual intuition, light from His Word, changed circumstances, or in some other way, we may realize that God has said no to us. By spiritual intuition, I mean that when God says no to a request, we have no peace in praying for it; it doesn't feel right; there is a sense of restraint.

Now let me speak to suggestions two and three, in the light of God's will.

God is more anxious for us to know His will than we are. For many people, finding God's will is a game of hide-and-seek, like hunting for green Easter eggs in tall grass. When someone asks me, "How do I find God's will?" my answer is, you don't. God's will finds you. It is not your responsibility to *find* or *discover* the will of God. If God wants you to know His will, it is His responsibility to reveal it—and reveal it in a way that you can't miss it.

Suppose I tell my daughter, Kimberly, that I have something I want her to do for me. She says she will and asks me what it is. "I'm not going to tell you," I say. "You have to figure it out on your own. And if you figure wrong, you're in trouble."

Ridiculous, isn't it? If I have a task for my child, it is my responsibility to reveal it. Her responsibility is to hear and obey.

In Romans 12:1,2, Paul tells us we can prove what the will of God is; we can look at two choices and discern which one is God's will. But first, he tells us to present ourselves to God, *present* meaning to submit or to yield.

Basically, Paul is saying that if we want to know God's will, we should accept it before we know what it is. The "tell me what it is and then I'll decide" stance never prevails with God. Knowing that God's will, whatever it is, is always best, we are to submit to it and accept it in advance.

How Will We Know?

Have you ever wished you had a spiritual referee around to tell you when you step out of bounds? Well, that's exactly what we do have. Listen to Colossians 3:15:

> And let the peace of God rule in your hearts, to which also you were called in one body; and be thankful.

Rule is the translation of a Greek word that means "to act as umpire." The Williams translation makes it clear: "Let the peace that Christ can give keep on *acting as umpire* in your hearts" (emphasis added).

Beck translates it, "Let the peace of Christ . . . be in your heart *to decide things* for you" (emphasis added).

Through Christ, the Christian has two kinds of peace: peace *with* God and the peace *of* God. Peace *with* God is the result of being justified by faith (Romans 5:1). The war between God and the Christian is over and the believer has been brought into a right relationship with God, a place of blessing. Peace with God is objective. Every believer possesses this regardless of his spiritual status. Nothing can disturb our peace with God.

The peace *of* God is God's peace, the peace that He Himself enjoys and shares with us. This peace is subjective, an inner calm and quiet assurance of the heart. The peace of God is the believer's heart at rest. Stepping outside the will of God disturbs this peace; our hearts become troubled, the quiet assurance disappears.

Paul is saying that we are to let the peace of Christ be the umpire in our lives, to let it decide what is right and wrong. When we lose that inner peace, when our heart is troubled and ill at ease, our spiritual umpire is blowing the whistle and calling a foul.

At times as I pray about a particular thing, there comes, suddenly or gradually, a check on my heart, a restraint. I don't feel right about it. In other words, I don't have peace about it. I take that as the umpire calling that prayer out of bounds.

The more sensitive we become to the Holy Spirit's leading, the more we will be able to discern the petitions that are and are not "according to the will of God."

A Prayer for Wisdom

I am reminded of a time when a great need arose in my own home. Symptoms of a manic depressive condition began to manifest themselves in our oldest son. (Later he was indeed diagnosed as manic depressive.) I'll not go into details except to say that for a while our world was a waking nightmare. Never had I felt so inadequate, so lost, so ignorant. Kaye and I claimed James 1:5 for ourselves:

> If any of you lacks wisdom, let him ask of God,
> who gives to all liberally and without reproach,
> and it will be given him.

And so we began to pray for wisdom when confronted with traumatic family decisions. But no wisdom came. There was no flash of brilliant insight, no swelling of wisdom in my head. I felt as dumbfounded as ever.

In my desperation I kept reading the verse over and over, trying to make myself believe it in spite of its obvious failure. I knew better than that, of course—it wasn't the promise that was failing. But what to do?

Then I saw it, as clear as my face in the mirror. The last phrase in the verse, the promise itself, says: "and it will be given to him." Period. Just like that.

If I asked God for wisdom, I must have it, whether I felt wise or not. Do you know what I did? I claimed the wisdom God had promised and then began making the decisions that *seemed best to me.* I believed I had the right to assume that, having asked God for wisdom, His wisdom was operating in me.

It was scary. At the time there was no way to know if my decisions were the "right" ones. Later, though, when that particular period was past, I could look back and see that in every instance I had made the right decision. God had kept His promise in answer to my praying.

Two concepts help me know when and how long to pray for something. **First**, I pray in the direction of my burden. That's the way I preach—in the direction of my burden. I preach what is "on my heart." This is one of the ways God leads us and we should learn to respond to the burden of our heart, believing that God has placed it there.

Second, I pray until the burden is lifted. As long as my heart is burdened about a thing, I will keep it before the Lord. When the burden is lifted, I'm released from that prayer.

*   *   *

P.S. I have mixed feelings about writing on "how" to pray. No one is really qualified to tell others how they should approach God in prayer. In this book, I've probably raised more questions than I have answered. There is always a "what if . . . ?" but I can't say everything in one book, so don't worry about it. Don't be intimidated by any "prayer plan" in this or any other book. Unanswered prayer is never a result of overlooked technicalities or violated protocol. Just do it. Jump out there and pray — the Holy Spirit will catch you and take you where you need to go.

A Praying Church in a Pagan World

It is reported that Mary, Queen of Scots, once said, "I fear the prayers of John Knox more than I fear all the armies on the face of the earth."

That was probably the last time anyone feared the prayers of the church.

It's hard to picture Yassar Arafat saying, "I fear the prayers of the saints more than I fear all the Uzis of Israel."

The world does not fear the church—it barely tolerates it. Generally, the world perceives the church as no longer a player in world affairs, only an observer, a "yes-man" for the pagan leaders of Western culture, a culture that has long since abandoned Christian presuppositions as a serious voice in shaping the values of modern society. The church is a quaint relic of the past that lends a certain charm to the neighborhood, a holdover from bygone days, big but harmless, like a beached whale.

For many, the most crucial question facing the church is whether it can survive. I can answer that question. Yes, the church will survive. God has never left Himself without a witness, and His church will still be around when the curtain comes down on this whole mess. It may not survive in its present form, but God help us if we're interested only in surviving. Christ intends that His church do a lot more.

The Age of Paganism

"The Post-Christian age is here." That is the opening statement of Harold Lindsell's book, *The New Paganism*.[1] His book shows that the Western world has been overcome by paganism. Lindsell writes:

> In the West the civilization based on Judeo-Christian foundations has collapsed. In its place, the West without exception lives and functions as a pagan world.[2]

The church is treading water in a sea of paganism, surrounded by a hostile world that hates New Testament Christianity and that wages an unrelenting war against it.

Whether we call the prevailing culture "paganism," "neo-paganism" or "secular humanism," one thing is clear: Our generation has witnessed what may be the final death blows to the Judeo-Christian foundation upon which most of the Western world was established.

An Earlier Age of Paganism

The prevailing climate is nothing new to the church. It was born in the midst of paganism, and it conquered it.

> Three hundred years after the beginning of Christ's public ministry, the church had brought the Roman Empire to its knees in worship of the Redeemer.[3]

How did that little band of eager disciples accomplish what no military power had been able to? Did they possess something that we do not? Did they know something that we do not?

The answer to those questions and others can be found in the record God has preserved of those pioneer Christians. A more revealing picture of the life and times of the early church can't be found than the one in the twelfth chapter of Acts.

The chapter opens with a bang:

> Now about that time Herod the King stretched out his hand to harass some from the church. Then he killed James the brother of John with the sword. And because he saw that it pleased the Jews, he proceeded further to seize Peter also. Now it was during the Days of Unleavened Bread (Acts 12:1-3).

Prayer and Peter's Release

Herod assigned sixteen soldiers to guard Peter, and Peter was bound by chains between two of them. For Peter there would be no escape, no reprieve.

> But constant prayer was offered to God for him by the church (verse 5).

The night before Peter was to be executed, an angel appeared in the prison where Peter was sleeping between his two guards. The angel woke Peter up and led him past the two guardposts, through the iron gate of the city, which opened automatically, and into a street, where the angel vanished as suddenly as he had appeared.

> And when Peter had come to himself, he said, "Now I know for certain that the Lord has sent His angel, and has delivered me from the hand of Herod and from all the expectation of the Jewish people."
>
> So, when he had considered this, he came to the house of Mary, the mother of John whose surname was Mark, where many were gathered together praying (verses 11,12).

Why didn't he run away? This panic-prone disciple had run before—when Jesus was on trial. He has an even better excuse now: His life *really is* in danger. Instead of fleeing, though, he goes to Mary's house where he knows the church is gathered. Later he will go into hiding, but first he must share with the church what God has done. Throughout the entire story (verses 1-19), we are struck by the calm control exercised by this former deserter.

The clue is in verse 12:

> So, *when he had considered this,* he came to the house of Mary.

Peter has matured. He stops and thinks before he runs. He considers what has just happened to him, then courageously and calmly goes to church.

Considering: Seeing Together

The word "considered" means *to see together.*
Peter took the recent events and put them together; he
saw them as a whole, not as isolated, unrelated happenings. If he had looked only at the death of James, he
might have fled; if he had looked only at the chains and
the guards, he might have panicked as before. He now
understood that everything in life is tied to something
else. No event occurs in isolation. Every thread is part
of the same fabric.

The same is true of us today. Many of the doom
and gloom assessments of the church's status are the
result of seeing things in isolation from other things. I
believe Christians need to consider, "to see together,"
all the happenings in our world. When we do, we shall
begin to become the Church Optimistic as well as the
Church Militant. I suggest that we consider, see together, four facts.

Fact 1: The church and the world are deadly enemies.

The old Isaac Watts hymn asked the question,
"Is this vile world a friend of grace, to help me on to
God?" The answer was no then, and it's still no. The
early church knew this. I'm not sure we do. I think
many still hope we can make up and become better
friends, or at least live in peaceful co-existence as good
neighbors.

I grew up in the Baptist church, and in those
days Baptists were pretty strict when it came to worldly
pleasures. We kids used to sing, "I don't smoke and I
don't chew, and I don't go with girls who do." One day,
I tried to get my mom's permission to go to a dance,

which was a major taboo. Patiently, she explained to me the great gulf between worldly pleasure and the Christian faith.

That was when I made my first attempt to join the worship of Jehovah to the worship of Baal. I asked, "How about if we dance to 'The Old Rugged Cross?' "

I'll never forget the look she gave me.

The enmity between the church and the world is enunciated by the apostle John when he says:

> Do not love the world or the things in the
> world. If anyone loves the world, the love of the
> Father is not in him. For all that is in the
> world—the lust of the flesh, the lust of the
> eyes, and the pride of life—is not of the Father
> but is of the world. And the world is passing
> away, and the lust of it; but he who does the
> will of God abides forever (1 John 2:15-17).

John uses the word *world* more often than all the other New Testament writers combined—seventy-nine times in his Gospel and twenty-three times in his first Epistle. The world that we are to shun is not the world of nature, the created order, the material universe. Nor is it the world of people, the human race, the world as a fallen world in need of grace. It is the world as a system organized without God, the unbelieving, pagan society, a society embodying the influences and forces hostile to God.

This world about which John warns us "is not made up of so many outward objects that can be specified; it is the sum of those influences emanating from men and things around us, which draw us away from God. It is the awful down-dragging current in life."[4] The world is human civilization organized and operating under the power of evil.

Alliance of Enemies of Christ

There's another aspect to this first fact of the church and the world being deadly enemies that needs to be noted: The enemies of Christ always unite.

When Herod killed James with the sword, he saw that it pleased the Jews, so he took steps to kill Peter also. Herod's actions were not motivated by great principles or deep convictions, but by a sorry desire to win the popularity of the Jews. The Jews were never fond of the Herods; the Herods were usurpers, and Edomite blood flowed in their veins. But this one, Herod Agrippa, grandson of Herod the Great, courted the Jews by keeping the Law and all the Jewish observances, even to the point of delaying Peter's execution until after the Passover. Herod and the Jews united against the church. Peter was killed by public opinion as much as by the sword.

This persecution under Herod Agrippa I was the third major attack on the apostles. The first was led by the Sadducees and the second by the Pharisees (Acts 4,6). Pharisees and Sadducees were cat-and-dog enemies. The Sadducees (the righteous ones) did not believe in the resurrection of the body or life after death, and they rejected rabbinic interpretation of the law.

The Pharisees (the separate ones) were legalists, concerned with ritual purity, tithing and strict observance of the law. Yet while these two groups were divided against each other, they were united against Christ (Matthew 16:11; 22:15-34). In Matthew 22:34, we read, "But when the Pharisees heard that He had silenced the Sadducees, they gathered together."

During Jesus' trial, when Pilate learned that Jesus was from Galilee, he sent him to Herod Antipas, who was ruler of Galilee and Peraea and had jurisdiction over the man from Galilee. Herod, after playing with Jesus, mocking Him and treating Him with contempt, sent Him back to Pilate. Luke adds this footnote to the incident:

> That very day Pilate and Herod became friends
> with each other, for before that they had been
> at enmity with each other (Luke 23:12).

When Pilate cried to the mob: "Shall I crucify your King?" they shouted back, "We have no King but Caesar!" (John 19:15)

A parallel in our day is how the *isms* have united against Christianity. Secularism has united with humanism, giving us secular humanism; liberalism has joined pluralism; Hedonism has blended into existentialism; and atheism has joined them all. To some, the *isms* may be nothing but abstract terms that have nothing to do with everyday life. Understandable — the postman and I hardly ever discuss existentialism, and I can't remember the last time I chit-chatted with someone about pluralism or relativism.

All this means that every major idea and philosophy shaping our world right now is opposed to New Testament Christianity and intends to wipe it from the face of the earth.

The church has imbibed more of these philosophies than it realizes, and much of its message and ministry is becoming an *ism* in sheep's clothing.

The real hope for our society is that the church will recapture its distinctiveness, that it will act instead of react and stop letting the world set its agenda. To the degree that we have lost that distinctiveness, we have lost our influence for Christ in the world. The more the church looks like the world, talks like the world or operates like the world, the more the world disdains it, for the world can beat the church at everything—except this: living out the life of Christ. That and that alone is our distinctiveness, and in that and that alone lies our power.

Fact 2: The success of evil is only apparent.

For years a leading newsman ended his report with the words, "And that's the way it is." A more accurate statement would have been, "And that's the way it *appears*."

Here is where "seeing together" is crucial. If you isolate the death of James and view it as a single, independent and unrelated event, you say, "Evil wins again. Once again God is out-maneuvered by the devil." But when you gather everything together and see it that way, you know differently. If God delivered Peter, then He could have delivered James; therefore, it only looks like God has been out-maneuvered.

Of course, this is one of the great tests of our faith, a test we do not always pass. Like the psalmist, when we see the prosperity of the wicked who "have more than heart could wish" (Psalm 73:7), we feel like saying, "Surely I have cleansed my heart in vain, and washed my hands in innocence" (verse 13). There is only one cure for this:

> When I thought how to understand this,
> It was too painful for me—
> *Until I went into the sanctuary of God;*
> *Then I understood their end*
>   (verses 16,17, emphasis added).

Listen to God as He speaks to our anxious hearts:

> Do not fret because of evil men
>   or be envious of those who do wrong;
> for like the grass they will soon wither,
>   like green plants they will soon die away . . .
> Do not fret when men succeed in their ways,
>   when they carry out their wicked schemes . . .
> For evil men will be cut off . . .
> A little while, and the wicked will be no more;
>   though you look for them, they will not be
>   found.
> But the meek will inherit the land
>   and enjoy great peace (Psalm 37:1-10, NIV).

Just as the guards looked for Peter and could not find him, the day is coming when we will look for the wicked and be unable to find them. When the upright get uptight they need to remember: The success of evil is only apparent.

Fact 3: God's hand, though unseen, is working.

We cannot always accurately interpret our situation; often outside circumstances contradict everything we believe. It is impossible to evaluate a situation on the basis of visible evidence. Philip, when asked by Jesus how they could feed the five thousand, answered from the viewpoint of the disciples' buying the food themselves. Like him, we dig into the pockets of our own resources and come up blank (John 6:5-7).[5]

Our God is often a silent and hidden God. Witness His unseen hand. The angel appears in the prison—the guards do not see him. A light illuminates the cell—the guards do not see it. The angel strikes Peter in the side, the chains fall off, and the guards do not hear their clatter on the stone. Peter straps on his sandals and clomps out of prison—the guards do not hear. Peter was long delivered before the guards realized he was gone.

For that matter, Peter was delivered before even he realized it. It was only after stepping into the street that he "came to himself" and knew he had been delivered.

Fact 4: The unseen hand of God is moved by prayer.

The response of the church to Peter's imprisonment is stated in Acts 12:5: "Peter was therefore kept in prison, *but constant prayer was offered to God for him by the church.*" The author of Acts would have us know that there was a vital connection between the deliverance of Peter and the prayers of the church.

I hesitate to say that God's hand *is moved by prayer,* because it almost sounds like I am infringing upon God's sovereignty. Yet in light of what we covered in the first two chapters, I think the wording is legitimate. Prayer does move the hand of God.

Instead of casting prayer as a polite nod to tradition or as a piece of pietistic irrelevance, we must see it as the true power of the church. The early church didn't have enough influence or prestige to get Peter out of prison, but they had enough power to pray him out. And even they did not know how strong they were, not believing Peter was standing at the door knocking.

The church has far more power than it knows. Much is being said and written today about the desperate need for an evangelical awakening like the one that came to England in the late eighteenth century under John Wesley. It was the influence of John Wesley and the Evangelical Revival, say historians, that spared England from a bloody revolution like the one that tore France apart.

J. Edwin Orr, in his remarkable book *The Eager Feet,* tells of the concert of prayer started by the Baptist Association of the Midlands, joined by the members of the Free Church, Methodists, Anglicans and other burdened believers. This concert of prayer paved the way not only for the general awakening, but also for the extraordinary outburst of missionary zeal in the last decade of the eighteenth century. Orr writes:

> It is significant that the union in prayer for a general revival preceded the French Revolution by a full seven years. The prevenient work of the Holy Spirit has often anticipated the onslaught of evil long before believers had become aware of the dangers that lay ahead.[6]

In his book, *England Before and After Wesley,* J. Wesley Bready comes to the conclusion that . . .

> the Evangelical Awakening was the true nursing-mother of the spirit and character values that have created and sustained Free Institutions throughout the English-speaking world.

Bready calls it "the moral watershed of Anglo-Saxon history."[7]

For most of my ministry I have been a student of revival and awakening and I have constantly run into one stubborn fact: In the recorded history of the church, there has never been a mighty outpouring of the Spirit in revival that did not begin in the persistent, prevailing prayers of desperate people. Revival has never come because men placed it on the calendar. It has come because God placed it in their hearts.

When the Church Prays

During the early years of this century God sent a mighty spiritual awakening to Wales, probably the greatest religious revival this century has witnessed. In a matter of months, thousands were miraculously converted, churches were packed with standing room only, and the moral character of village after village was transformed. News of the strange and inexplicable happenings spread throughout the world, and many traveled to this obscure little country to observe God at work.

One night in one of the churches, Evan Roberts, the unofficial leader of the revival, called for testimonies from the congregation. A man stood and identified himself as an evangelist from another country. He said, "I have come to Wales to glean the secret of the Welsh revival."

Instantly, Roberts thrust his finger toward the visitor and shouted, "There is no secret! Ask and you shall receive!"

I wonder if the evangelist was disappointed with that answer. I think I would have been. After all, prayer is no secret. It's certainly not anything new. I pray every day and my church has prayer meetings every Wednesday night. But nothing like that ever happens. There must be something else, a program, a formula, a unique twisting of the ordinary — a secret. I doubt if any of us would have accepted Evan Roberts's statement as the real explanation of the revival. Oh, we would agree that prayer is important, but we would quickly add, "Besides prayer, what else did you do?"

The "Secret"

Yet, Evan Roberts was right. There is no secret. It *is* "ask and you shall receive." That is what we have not done. We put together our own recipe for revival, and after we mix together all our man-made ingredients, we add a dash of prayer for flavor. Real prayer, the kind that opens heaven's floodgates, the "wrestling" that Paul speaks of in Romans 15:30 — we know little or nothing of that kind of praying.

What could we expect to happen if the church returned to its kneeling posture and recovered its prayer power? We have seen one picture in Acts 12; now let's focus on the praying church in Acts 4.

The apostles have just had their first head-on collision with the Sanhedrin, a confrontation brought about by the healing of a lame man (Acts 3). When the people saw the former cripple walking, leaping and praising God, they mobbed Peter and John, and Peter seized the opportunity to preach Christ to them. He told the people that Jesus had been crucified, had been raised from the grave, and was truly both Lord and Christ. In Acts 4 we see that the priests and Sadducees, angered by Peter's talk of resurrection, grabbed Peter, along with John, and threw them both in jail.

The next day the Sanhedrin, after threatening Peter and John, commanded them not to speak or teach in the name of Jesus, and then they released them from custody. Immediately, the two disciples returned to the gathered believers and related the story. What was the young church's reaction?

Did they try to establish a dialogue with the Sanhedrin or organize a protest march against religious discrimination? No. This young body of believers, faced with its first opposition, went to its knees.

What happened when the church prayed is recorded in Acts 4:31:

> And when they had prayed, the place where
> they were assembled together was shaken; and
> they were all filled with the Holy Spirit, and
> they spoke the word of God with boldness.

The Presence of God Perceived

"The place . . . was shaken." This expression symbolizes God's active presence. A similar phrase occurs in Acts 16:26. In Philippi, Paul and Silas had been beaten and thrown into prison, and their feet were fastened into stocks. At midnight those two missionaries began to pray and sing hymns, and . . .

> suddenly there was a great earthquake, so that
> the foundations of the prison were shaken; and

immediately all the doors were opened and
everyone's chains were loosed.

This was the manifestation of God's presence,
declaring that He was there and that He was acting.

Isn't God always present when two or three
gather in His name? That is true, but God also can be
present without our knowledge. At Bethel, after seeing
the manifestation of God in the angels ascending and
descending on a ladder stretching from earth to heaven,
Jacob said,

Surely the Lord is in this place, and I did not
know it (Genesis 28:16).

That could be the theme song of many a Sunday
morning worship service.

We do always have the presence of God. What
we do not always have, however, is the awareness of His
presence. Vance Havner used to say that when we
preachers look out upon our small remnant and quote,
"Where two or three are gathered together in My name,
there am I in the midst of them," we usually are more
conscious of the absence of the people than the presence
of the Lord.

God's presence often is not real to us. We sometimes speak of Him as though He were absent. We pray
that way. Have you ever listened to prayers, to your own
prayers? We sometimes speak to God in the third person, as though we were talking to the congregation
rather than praying to God.

But when the church abandons itself to prayer,
the presence of God is perceived. Suddenly we know He
is there, working, moving, answering.

That is enough. It is enough to know He is on the scene. Let the Sanhedrin rant and rave; let them threaten; let them condemn. God is with us, and that is enough. In the face of insurmountable difficulties, the assurance of His presence is sufficient.

Atmospheric Revival

This perceived presence — an atmosphere that is charged with the obvious presence of God in such a way people know He is there — is a common characteristic of great revivals. During the Welsh revival it was reported that strangers entering the villages, unaware of the awakening, would suddenly fall under deep conviction and seek out a minister to pray for them. Fishermen, drawing near to shore, again unaware of the revival, would come under terrible conviction of sin and, before their feet touched land, every man on board would be converted.

It was said of Charles Finney that during times of revival he could walk down a street and passers-by would literally be thrown to their knees under the weight of conviction. Into every city Finney went, a man called Father Nash accompanied him, and he would closet himself in a room to do nothing but intercede for Finney and the meetings.

I have witnessed this "atmospheric revival" a few times — times when the presence of God was so thick you could cut it with a knife. People driving onto the church parking lot and falling immediately under conviction, people calling in the middle of the night, unable to wait until morning, asking how to be saved, people making restitution and seeking reconciliation —

all these things and more attended the "atmospheric revival."

In the early 1950s this kind of revival came to our city, under the ministry of my home church and its pastor. Everywhere I went in town—on a city bus, in the park, at school—I heard people talking about it. Not all good talk, but talk. You couldn't escape the confrontation. It was said that to escape the "atmosphere" you had to get at least a hundred miles away. I remember standing, as a teenager, on the steps outside the church, praying and confessing my sins. I wasn't about to walk in there without being right with God.

It would be a mistake to take these, or any examples, and make them the "norm" for God's manifestation. I've been in some churches that shook, not by the presence of God, but by loud preaching and blaring amplifiers. Shaking buildings is not our business, nor is it our task to produce signs of His presence. When the Lord shakes the building you don't have to announce it.

In extraordinary times God does extraordinary things—but He is just as much in the ordinary. The God who raised Jesus from the grave is the same God who raises the sun every morning.

United Prayer

One other thing: The Bible says this praying church "raised their voice to God with one accord" (Acts 4:24). This is an eloquent statement of the church's oneness, both in their action and their motive. It wasn't just the apostles who prayed. They all prayed. Here was a group of believers who gathered in one place to do one thing with one motive. This is a testimony to united prayer.

While there is power in the prayers of one person, the Bible indicates there is something special about united prayer. Jesus said,

> Again I say to you that if two of you agree on earth concerning anything that they ask, it will be done for them by My Father in heaven (Matthew 18:19).

The church was in one accord, like the men of Israel who came together to make David king:

> All these men of war, who could keep ranks, came to Hebron with a loyal heart, to make David king over all Israel; and all the rest of Israel were of one mind to make David king (1 Chronicles 12:38).

That is the kind of praying that shakes a place — when God's people come together with one heart to make Jesus king. When all our different concerns are thrust aside and our hearts flow into one main stream — that's when the presence of God is manifested and people know God has taken the field.

The Power of God Received

"And when they prayed . . . they were all filled with the Holy Spirit" (Acts 4:31). They were *all* filled, the record states. Not the apostles only, but every member of the church experienced the Spirit's filling. There had been such a filling on the day of Pentecost but the church can't run on the fumes of a previous fill-up. Every new task demands a fresh fullness.

There is something remarkable about this incident. As a result of their praying, they were all filled with the Holy Spirit — but examine the prayer. The Holy Spirit isn't mentioned; to be filled with the Spirit was not part of the petition. They didn't pray to be filled with the Spirit but when they prayed they were filled with the Spirit. Two things are significant.

One, they were not seeking an experience. There was nothing selfish or subjective about their petition. They weren't after the "thrill of the fill." I have witnessed a strange transition during my ministry. It used to be that Christians wanted the fullness of the Spirit for power — power to serve Christ and power to live for Him. Now we seem to act as though the purpose of being filled is not power in serving, but pleasure in living. The goal of it all is to feel good and have tremendous ecstatic experiences. I'm afraid many of us are more interested in the "feeling of the Spirit" than the filling of the Spirit.

Two, these verses show that there is more to being filled with the Spirit than merely asking for it. As a matter of fact, we don't have to ask God to fill us in order to be filled. The New Testament doesn't tell of anyone actually asking to be filled with the Spirit. Luke 11:13 comes close:

> If you then, being evil, know how to give good
> gifts to your children, how much more will your
> heavenly Father give the Holy Spirit to those
> who ask Him!

I am not saying we should not pray to be filled. We can, but it isn't necessary.

If we examine the content of the early church's prayer we may discover the kind of praying that results in the filling of the Spirit.

1. They recognized God as sovereign.

In Acts 4:24 we read:

So when they heard that, they raised their
voice to God with one accord and said: "Lord,
You are God, who made heaven and earth and
the sea, and all that is in them."

The word translated "Lord" here is rare. It is
not the same word rendered "Lord" in verse 29. In verse
24 it is an extremely strong word meaning "despot."
The word *despot* usually has a negative connotation,
but here it indicates God's omnipotence, His rule with
absolute and unrestrained authority.

This is where they started — not with the threats
of the enemy but with the absolute authority of God.
For the church, victory always begins with the recogni-
tion that God is our Sovereign Lord.

His sovereignty is seen in His creation of all
things. They acknowledged God as the creator of "heav-
en and earth and the sea, and all that is in them." Why?
Because they had a problem with some of the "all that
is in them." The Sanhedrin were creatures and God had
created them. The people in this church looked beyond
the creation to the creator, beyond the visible to the
invisible. One of the favorite threats kids use against
each other is, "I'm going to tell on you!" Well, that's
what these Christians did -- they told on the Sanhedrin.
Part of the creation was troubling them and they ap-
pealed to the creator.

His sovereignty is also seen in His control of all
things. Look again at their prayer. They began by
quoting from Psalm 2:

"The kings of the earth took their stand,
And the rulers were gathered together

> Against the LORD and against His Christ."
> For truly against Your holy Servant Jesus,
> whom You anointed, both Herod and Pontius
> Pilate, with the Gentiles and the people of Is-
> rael, were gathered together (Acts 4:26,27).

Look at the powers gathered against Christ: kings and rulers, Herod and Pilate, the Gentiles and Israel. But that's not the end. They go on:

> To do whatever Your hand and Your purpose
> determined before to be done (verse 28).

These persecuted believers looked back at the darkest day of their lives, the day their hopes and dreams disintegrated with the death of Christ, and saw *God in charge of it all.* And if it was true with the crucifixion of their Lord, how much more so with the persecution of His disciples. That was a magnificent display of His absolute sovereignty.

2. They recognized themselves as God's servants.

In verse 29 they refer to themselves as servants, as bond-slaves:

> Now, Lord, look on their threats, and grant to
> Your servants *that with all boldness they may
> speak Your word* (emphasis added).

This was a prayer of submission. They didn't complain about the circumstances or call down fire from heaven on the Sanhedrin. Nor did they beg God to move them to a more favorable situation. They simply asked God for more of what had gotten them into trouble in the first place—boldness: "Now when they saw the boldness of Peter and John . . . " (Acts 4:13). They submitted to God-allowed circumstances.

They also submitted to their God-appointed commission. The plea of the prayer in verse 29 is that they will have the boldness to continue doing what God had called them to do — speaking the Word and glorifying Jesus.

Now let's put it all together. In their prayer, which brought about a fresh supply of the power of God, they (1) acknowledged God as the sovereign Lord, and (2) submitted to Him and His redemptive purpose. I believe it is safe to say that any Christian who acknowledges and submits to the lordship of Jesus Christ is filled with the Holy Spirit. These conditions for being filled with the Holy Spirit assume, of course, a personal purity, a consistent pattern of cleansing through confession of sin.

When the Holy Spirit finds a believer who wants what He wants, they "get together." The Spirit is interested in one thing — glorifying Jesus as Lord and Savior. And He is ready to fill any Christian through whom He can do that.

The Purpose of God Achieved

Acts 4:33 contains two noteworthy phrases: "great power" and "great grace." This band of believers possessed great power to *do* what God wanted and great grace to *be* what God wanted — empowered witnesses with enriched lives.

Empowered witnesses

"And they spoke the word of God with boldness" (verse 31). Notice the chain reaction: When a church is filled with the Holy Spirit it will inevitably speak the word of God with boldness. We cannot divorce the fullness of the Spirit from witnessing. To be filled with the Spirit is to allow the Holy Spirit to express Himself through us, to carry out His commission through our lives. And unless we are willing to be instruments of His purpose it is useless to pray for His help.

When I use the term "witness" I am not referring to any particular method of witnessing. I don't mean that if you're filled with the Holy Spirit you will preach on street corners—you may or you may not. It is for the Spirit to say how, when and where we witness; but our lives, in one way or another, will witness of the Lord Jesus Christ when we are yielded to the Spirit.

It is worth our time to mark some of the features of this witness.

Obligation. With great power the apostles "gave" witness. The word translated "gave" means to give back, to return; it conveys the idea of repaying a debt or fulfilling an obligation. We are not doing God a favor when we share Christ with others. We are paying a debt. It is something we are obligated to do. The Holy Spirit makes a person honest, and an honest person always pays his debts. Paul expressed this same sense of obligation to the Romans: "I am a debtor both to Greeks and to barbarians, both to wise and to unwise" (Romans 1:14).

Boldness. They spoke the word of God with "boldness." *Boldness* is one of the great words of the New Testament. Again and again God uses this word to characterize the lives and ministries of New Testament believers. As used in the New Testament, boldness contains *three shades of meaning:*

(1) It means *courage to speak,* especially in the presence of men of high rank. The immediate example of this, of course, is the transformation of Peter from a

cowering Christ-denier to the fearless preacher of Pentecost. In churches across the country I have asked Christians the main problem they had with witnessing to a lost person. The leading answer is always fear. But the Spirit gives us courage to speak.

(2) It means *clarity of speech,* the ability to make clear and plain the message of Christ. The Holy Spirit can give us the ability to express ourselves, to make our witness understood.

(3) It means *confidence in what we speak.* This is the heart-assurance that what we say will be driven home by the Spirit. Though we may see no visible signs, we know our words penetrate the heart and the seed of the gospel is sown.

What was this witness that they gave with great power? "And with great power the apostles gave witness to the resurrection of the Lord Jesus" (Acts 4:33). Our message is that Jesus is living and that He is Lord. This brings us back to where we started. When the place is shaken and the presence of God is perceived, it's not difficult to convince men that Jesus is alive and that He is Lord.

When the Philippian jailer stood amidst the rubble of his demolished jail, saw the prison doors hanging on broken hinges, heard Paul and Silas singing hymns and praising God, and saw that all the prisoners were still there, he was convinced—and he cried out, "What must I do to be saved?" (see Acts 16:25-30). He wasn't a prospect for the God-is-dead movement—he had perceived the presence of God.

It is hard to convince an atheistic age like ours to believe that Jesus is alive and reigning if they see little evidence to support our claim. At Pentecost, Peter pointed to the manifestation of the Holy Spirit as proof that Jesus was both Lord and Christ, sitting at the right hand of God (Acts 2:33).

Enriched lives

"And great grace was upon them all" (Acts 4:33). Can you think of a more eloquent description of this community of unity?

A part of this great grace was surely the harmony of the fellowship described by the phrase, "one heart and one soul" (verse 32). Many believers but one body, beating with one heart, thinking with one mind, feeling with one soul. The most ignorant sinner in town knows that the mark of Christianity is unity. It is precisely this, Jesus said, that shows the world that the Father sent Him . . .

> that they all may be one, as You, Father, are in Me, and I in You; that they also may be one in Us, that the world may believe that You sent me (John 17:21).

Another part of the great grace that was upon the church is expressed in these words:

> Neither did anyone say that any of the things he possessed was his own, but they had all things in common. . . . Nor was there anyone among them who lacked; for all who were possessors of lands or houses sold them, and brought the proceeds of the things that were sold, and laid them at the apostles' feet; and they distributed to each as anyone had need (Acts 4:32-35).

This is what happens to a praying church: The Holy Spirit baptizes it with a new concept, a changed viewpoint. The members have a new sense of respon-

sibility toward one another, and they see their possessions as a trust given by God to be used as needed among
the family. Did you know there was no such thing as a
needy person in that church? "There were no needy
persons among them," reads the NIV (verse 34).

Party causes, petty claims, little ownerships and
narrow boundaries were carried away by the flow of the
Spirit, and hand joined heart as the church cared for
both the spiritual and the social needs of one another.
And, in reality, the two cannot be severed, for the
witness of one makes believable the witness of the
other. The twin spirals of smoke ascending to the Father come from the same sweet-smelling sacrifice.

This is the New Testament picture of a praying
church in a pagan world. The church must learn to live
in a kneeling position, for in order to pray for revival,
there first must be a revival of praying.

Appendix A

Planning an Intercessory Prayer Ministry

So I sought for a man among them who would
make up a wall and STAND IN THE GAP before
Me on behalf of the land, that I should not
destroy it; but I found no one (Ezekiel 22:30).

When we started our intercessory prayer ministry in
1972 we had only a conviction that we should and a commitment that we would. We had no knowledge of a similar prayer
ministry to use as a guide and as far as we knew, there was
nothing in print to help us. We made it up as we went along.

In the next few years, we helped other churches
establish prayer ministries—including a Catholic church. A
member of our staff helped set up the prayer ministry of one
of the largest Christian organizations in the world. Each
church and each organization adjusted the plan to fit its own
situation. There is no one right way to do it.

Staffing a 24-hours-a-day, 7-days-a-week prayer
ministry may be impossible for your church—you may not
have that many members. Then have a 3-hours-a-day, 4-
days-a-week prayer ministry—there's nothing sacrosanct
about 24 hours or 7 days. Start where you are and expand as
you grow. Something is better than nothing.

Even the smallest church can have a prayer ministry
when the people experience a conviction and develop a sense
of commitment. Let me encourage you not to be intimidated
by the expanse of our organization. Ours started very small,
and grew with the growth of the ministry and the availability

of people to make up the staff. Just take what will be helpful to you from the following information, and use it or adapt it to whatever form works for you. This is simply an explanation as to how we do it, and is offered as a suggestion for your use.

I have taken this appendix out and replaced it at least a dozen times. Right now as I write this I am tempted to remove it—because I'm not sure you can start a prayer ministry by organizing one. Maybe you can, maybe you can't; I don't know. As I mentioned in the introduction, we did not organize our prayer ministry in order to create a prayer ministry—we organized the ministry after it arrived. There is a great difference between the two.

PREPARING THE CHURCH FOR A MINISTRY OF INTERCESSION

To the PASTOR: You are the key.

You may be more of a people-oriented person and not so good with organizational details as this program might seem to require. The answer to that dilemma is for you to be the motivator and to have someone else, someone who is good at it, manage the organizing. Here is what you need to do:

I. You must be a man of prayer. Immerse yourself in the subject.

    A. Give priority to prayer in your own life.

    B. Read yourself full of good books on prayer (see bibliography).

    C. Start an "Answered Prayer" book. Record the history of your Asking and Answering experiences.

    D. Do a topical study of prayer in the Bible.

II. Preach from your overflow on prayer and intercession.

    A. Impress upon your people the priority of prayer.

    B. Teach the various aspects of prayer: petition, confession, meditation, etc.

    C. Share with the congregation answers you have received.

    D. Preach a series of messages specifically on intercessory praying.

III. Plan some weekend retreats for couples, single adults, etc.

    A. Tell them the object of the retreat is to learn how to pray.

    B. Find a good resource book to teach at the retreat. The book I taught to each group first was *Teaching Conversational Prayer* by Rosalind Rinker. The concept of "conversational prayer" freed my people. Some who had never prayed aloud in a group did so with ease and joy once they found they didn't have to compose and deliver a long prayer with the "thees" and "thous" in the right places.

    C. Spend some time actually praying together.

IV. Challenge the church to a day of intercession.

    A. Pray at the church.

    B. Pray from 8 A.M. Saturday through 8 A.M. Sunday.

    C. Place a large chart divided into 24 hours in a convenient location and ask people to sign up for at least one hour.

    D. Do not appoint leaders for the prayer times. Let the people come to the areas designated (usually the sanctuary), pick their own spot and pray by themselves or join someone else if they want to. The point is to let them learn that they can pray on their own, without a leader telling them when and what to pray for and how long. They must become "self-starters."

    E. Have several Bibles available along with "Preparing to Pray" sheets (a sample is included) plus several copies of a small list of specific requests—just three

or four general requests related to the church and
the approaching worship services.

V. In the following Sunday evening service give people
an opportunity to share what the day of intercession
meant to them.

VI. Challenge them to start a 24-hour Ministry of
Intercession.

Do not be in a hurry to start the "official" prayer
ministry. Patience is a virtue here. Give God time to
work prayer as a priority into the life of your church.

Don't ask the people to *vote* on this. Just announce
that the church is starting a ministry of intercession and
that you will trust God to supply the intercessors. Note:
We never tried to recruit intercessors—we preferred
they volunteer.

BEGINNING YOUR MINISTRY OF INTERCESSION

I. Provide a PRAYER CHAPEL.

A. You will need a **place to pray,** so set apart a specific place in your church as the Prayer Chapel.
This place will be used *exclusively* for prayer.

B. The Prayer Chapel must be situated in such a way
that it can be used 24 hours a day, 7 days a week.
In our existing buildings there was no place
available so we built one. It is an attractive frame
building sitting next to our educational building.
The chapel should be a comfortable size. Ours is
14 feet by 16 feet.

C. The Prayer Chapel should be **furnished com-
fortably,** attractively and functionally.

1. We built a **prayer rail** across the front of the
chapel with a counter behind it wide enough to
hold the telephone, answering machine, Rolodex,
request books, etc. A thick red cushion covers

the kneeling rail. (There's nothing spiritual about sore knees).

2. You may want to install an answering machine in the chapel so people can phone in requests at any time.

3. An electric clock.

4. An electric heat/air conditioning unit independent of the other buildings since the chapel may be open when other buildings are not in use.

5. A table near the entrance with a sign-in book.

6. Request books, Answer Box and Rolodex (more about these in the Prayer Manual).

7. Several Bibles in different translations.

8. Several "Preparing to Pray" sheets (see Prayer Manual), laminated for longer use.

9. Provide maps of the world, the United States and your city, with colored pins designating the location of the people and churches you are praying for.

II. You will need a PRAYER STAFF to care for the organizational aspects of the prayer ministry. This is a good place to remind you that you will have to adjust these plans for your own church. Don't be daunted by details that may be irrelevant to your situation.

A. A GENERAL CHAIRMAN. This must be someone who is readily available, preferably a church staff member. He or she will:

1. Appoint a Prayer Secretary (described below).

2. Enlist and supervise the fourteen coordinators.

3. Deal with problem requests. Occasionally a request comes in that is an obvious prank, or too personal, or in bad taste. Your intercessors may be asked to pray for something contrary to your church's doctrinal and ethical convictions. It

happened to us. These are not to be placed on the Rolodex. The General Chairman will make the decision.

4. Some of the requests will need to be reworded for the sake of clarification and brevity. Remember the request must fit on a small Rolodex card.

In a word, the General Chairman will supervise the entire ministry of intercession. He is not to do all the work; he is to see that it gets done. He must believe strongly in intercession and be committed without reservation to its ministry in your church.

B. A PRAYER SECRETARY. A ministry of intercession cannot function properly without this key person. Before we entered this ministry we had no idea of the time and work that would be involved in keeping it running efficiently. You cannot afford to skimp here. There is nothing as discouraging to an Intercessor as finding out he's been praying for weeks for an out-of-date request.

If your church is able to hire a secretary, great! If not, ask God to give you someone within your fellowship to take this position. When we started our ministry, one of our secretaries added this to her responsibilities—it didn't take long to realize the load was too heavy. Soon we had six volunteers who each gave one hour a week of secretarial duty to the ministry. This relieved the work load of the Prayer Secretary and still allowed the ministry to function through the church office (which is important).

Functions of the Prayer Secretary:

1. Check the Chapel each morning on the hour or during a vacant hour (this prevents disturbing an Intercessor).

   a. Pick up completed sign-in sheets. These are mailed *daily* to Coordinators along with stamped absentee cards for those who missed their hour.

b. Take messages off answering machine and place in appropriate request book, i.e., **Emergency** or **Immediate Request** (see page 4 of manual).

c. Remove every Emergency Request that is seven days old.

d. Remove all but one sheet (the present day's) of requests from the Immediate Request ledger.

e. Check the Answer Box (see page 3 of manual for answers, notes, suggestions, updates, etc.)

f. See that there is an adequate supply of forms in all notebooks, scratch pads, pencils, Kleenex, etc. Straighten the Chapel.

2. Process the requests.

a. Transfer new requests from the Immediate Request notebook to a MASTER REQUEST BOOK which is to be kept in the church office.

b. Type a Rolodex card for each request and place it in the Rolodex in the Chapel.

c. These requests are then indexed in a card file kept in the office by name and number. This index makes it easy to locate answers or requests for people and eliminates duplication.

3. Keep Prayer Chart (see paragraph V, item B) updated.

This Prayer Chart is the **MASTER LISTING** of all Intercessors. It is kept up to date as Intercessors are added or removed, or as their hours are changed.

4. Secure Reserves for Intercessors who cannot meet their hour or are unable to reach their Coordinator.

5. Notify coordinators of changes within their twelve-hour period.

6. Be responsible for supply/printing of all forms used in the ministry.

7. Be responsible for updating the Rolodex (see V under *Maintaining the Ministry of Intercession*).

Of course, you will have to tailor this to your own situation, but don't let the size of the task scare you off. Do not let anything discourage you from making your church a House of Prayer.

C. 14 PRAYER COORDINATORS. These men and women will be responsible for twelve one-hour periods each. They will have a list of their Intercessors and the hour they pray.

The Coordinators have two duties:

1. Provide a Reserve Intercessor when one of their Regular Intercessors is unable to meet his hour. Each coordinator will have a list of Reserve Intercessors and upon receiving word that a Regular will be absent, starts at the top and calls until he finds one who can fill that hour. If he is unable to get a Reserve, he informs the Prayer Secretary. For the next call, he will start where he left off with the last call.

2. Weekly, the Prayer Secretary will furnish him with a list of his Regulars who missed their hour. If the absentee fails to notify his coordinator, the coordinator will send him a card provided by the church office (sample card in Appendix B, fig. 3).

V. Enlist your INTERCESSORS. Your ultimate goal is two intercessors for every hour, or 336. Don't be discouraged if you don't reach it the first month — we never did reach it!

Age limit. Intercessors, Regular or Reserve, must be at least 16 years old. There are several reasons for this age requirement:

—Many Intercessors will be praying alone late at night and in the early hours of the morning.

—The Intercessors must be mature enough to use good telephone manners and convey a feeling of confidence to the caller.

—Many of the requests are extremely personal and confidential. This is too much responsibility to place on immature shoulders.

You will want to enlist two kinds of Intercessors:

A. REGULAR INTERCESSORS. These will sign up for at least one hour a week (i.e., Monday, 1-2 P.M.) and will fill this hour every week until Jesus comes, or they die, move out of town, change to another hour, or backslide. We encourage Intercessors to sign up in pairs. Having a partner encourages faithfulness and enriches their prayer time. Many husbands and wives share the same hour.

B. RESERVE INTERCESSORS. Some will have work schedules that prohibit a commitment to a specific hour. These people may serve as Reserve Intercessors. When a Regular cannot fill his hour, he will notify his Coordinator, who will in turn contact a Reserve to fill the vacancy. The Reserve will be on call at all times, even though he may not be able to serve every time he is asked.

Regulars may want to serve as Reserves also. Many find that praying just an hour isn't enough and welcome the opportunity to spend another hour in intercession. You will need many Reserve Intercessors, especially during the vacation months.

Enlist your Intercessors by placing in a convenient location a large PRAYER CHART that has been divided into days and hours. Have your Prayer Secretary be available before and after the worship services to sign up people. Do not let the people sign up by themselves. The secretary will want to fill out a card for the office files for each person who signs the large Chart.

The period of intense enlistment should last for a month. After that, they can sign up in the church office.

VI. Have an INTERCESSORY PRAYER CLINIC for all Regulars, Reserves and anyone else who is interested in the ministry to go through the procedure of praying in the Chapel.

    A. Repeat the Clinic so those who are unable to attend one will have an additional opportunity. We found Sunday afternoon to be the best time for us.

    B. Make a tape recording of the Clinic to loan to new Intercessors as they are enlisted.

    C. Have the sign-up Prayer Chart available at the clinic.

    D. Use the *Intercessory Prayer Manual* (Appendix B) as your teaching guide. It is best if each person has a copy.

    E. Dramatize an hour in the Chapel. Show them step by step what to do, from the moment they walk through the door until the moment they leave.

    F. Give opportunity for questions. A clear understanding is a MUST.

    G. Have a prayer of commitment.

    H. Invite them to visit the Prayer Chapel as they leave.

MAINTAINING THE MINISTRY
OF INTERCESSION

"Watch and pray" is the key, with emphasis on *watch*. Satan trembles at the sight of a praying church and will do everything he can to destroy your ministry of intercession. People's indifference, neglect and discouragement are his most effective weapons. As a shepherd maintains constant vigil over his flock, so you must watch over this ministry. Here are some things we found helpful in maintaining the ministry of intercession.

I. Meet with your Coordinators every three months. At this meeting:

A. Review God's blessings on the ministry.

B. Report on the number of requests, answers, Intercessors, etc.

C. Have a time for questions and answers—and suggestions. This will help you work out the "bugs."

D. Spend time praying for the ministry and the ministers.

II. At least once a year, plan an INTERCESSORY PRAYER CONFERENCE.

This can be a valuable time of information and inspiration as well as a time for enlisting the newer members of your church in the prayer ministry.

A. Plan to meet for this conference on a Friday night and Saturday morning. It is good to invite someone outside your church who is well-qualified to speak on the subject to lead the conference.

B. Have two forty-five minute sessions on Friday night with a fifteen-minute break in between. Light refreshments can be served.

Make this Friday-night session a time of inspiration and information. In no other area of Christian living is the statement, "The spirit is willing but the flesh is weak," more true than in the prayer life.

This two-part Friday-night session should present a Spirit-anointed challenge to the people to "pray always and not faint."

C. On Saturday morning:

9-9:30 – Meet with the Coordinators to discuss any problems or suggestions.

9:30-10:30 – Meet in the auditorium for a training session in which you re-introduce the Ministry of Intercession, share the blessings of the past year, and relate any problems that need correcting. Then go through the procedure of praying in the Chapel, just as you did in the original Clinic.

10:30-10:45 – Break for refreshments.

10:45-11:45 – Have a closing message dealing with the spiritual qualifications of an Intercessor.

After the conference have the Prayer Secretary available to sign up new Intercessors.

III. Every three months, mail a PRAISE NEWSLETTER to all the Intercessors, Regular and Reserve. This letter should list all the requests that have been answered and any other information pertinent to the ministry. Include a testimony from one or two Intercessors of how the ministry has blessed them personally. Actually, it would be good to mail this newsletter to the entire church membership.

IV. Keep the ministry before the church.

A. In your mid-week worship service, share testimonies of the blessings of being a part of the ministry as well as prayers answered.

B. Publicize the phone number of the Prayer Chapel in the Sunday bulletin, church paper and local newspaper.

C. Each week, publish in the church bulletin or newsletter the hours still unfilled. Ask the church to pray that God will supply needed Intercessors.

D. **This is special.** When someone whose name was on the intercessory prayer list makes a public decision (joins the church, receives Christ as Savior, etc.), let the congregation know that this is the fruit of the ministry. You may even want to ask those who remember praying for that person to stand. This is a powerful testimony to the church and an encouragement to the Intercessors, as well as to the one who was prayed for.

V. Keep the requests up to date.

An undependable request list cripples the confidence of your Intercessors.

A. Always get the **source** of the request. When someone phones in a request, ask for the name, address and phone number of the party calling. Ask the person to keep you informed of any changes in the situation. Occasionally, a caller will want to remain anonymous. Assure him that the information will be confidential. If the caller still refuses to identify himself, assure him that you understand and that his request will be taken care of. You are there to help, and while it is important to have this information, it's not important enough to turn anyone away from the ministry. Gently and courteously ask him to keep you informed of the situation.

When the request comes in by letter, answer immediately, informing the writer that his request has been added to the prayer list and asking him to keep you informed about the situation.

B. Each month remove the **pink** cards from the Rolodex (see page 3 of the Prayer Manual).

C. Every six months review the **blue** cards (see page 3 of the Prayer Manual).

1. Take out the requests for *physical healing*
   and update the information. If you do not know
   the source of the request and can find no current information regarding the person prayed
   for, we recommend that it be removed from the
   Rolodex. (You will still have a record of the request in the Master Request Book in the church
   office.)

   If this seems harsh, imagine that you have 500
   requests. The time in the Prayer Chapel is precious and you will quickly realize that it isn't fair
   to the Intercessors to ask them to pray over a
   request that may be invalid.

   I mention physical healing because, next to
   salvation, these probably will be the most fre-
   quent requests made.

2. Do the same with the other **blue** card requests
   dealing with home problems, employment, etc.
   Try to update but **do not remove salvation**
   requests at this time.

3. After **one year**, remove the **salvation** requests
   that have not and cannot be updated.

D. Once a year, update the **white** cards. These are permanent requests but pastors will have moved,
   missionaries will have been transferred, etc.

   Note: We found that Intercessors often get discouraged praying for the same request week after
   week for six months or a year. All they see is a name
   on a card — they probably don't know the person and
   may never know him. Seeing the same old request
   for a year without any new information, they have
   a right to wonder if the request is valid or the
   information correct. On the other hand, if they know
   that every request is being constantly updated and
   are assured that every card represents a valid and
   current need, they will pray with joy and confidence.

Appendix B

THE INTERCESSORY PRAYER MANUAL

Dear Intercessor:

Welcome to God's greatest adventure! You are entering the highest work any person can do for God and the greatest thing you can do for others. Get ready to see God do exceeding abundantly above all that you ask or think, and remember what He said: "If you ask anything in My name, I will do it." As you release the power of God through prayer in Jesus' name, people all over the world will be blessed, and God will be glorified.

PREPARATION

Intercession is more than something you do at 9 A.M. every Tuesday. It is a way of life (Romans 1:9). Intercession is God's key to the Christian that unlocks the storehouse of heaven (Matthew 7:11). It is the means God uses to work in the lives of others (Job 42:10).

Because intercession is a way of life, the ministry of intercession should not be entered into carelessly. Your involvement must come from a . . .

CLEAR CALL

Jesus taught that men always ought to pray (Luke 18:1). The prophets reported that God's judgment on His people was determined by the presence or absence of intercessors (Jeremiah 5:1; Ezekiel 22:30,31). Samuel considered neglecting to pray for others a sin (1 Samuel 12:23).

CLEAN LIFE

David answers his own haunting question:

Who shall ascend into the hill of the LORD?
  or who shall stand in His holy place?
He that hath clean hands, and a pure heart;
  who hath not lifted up his soul unto vanity,
  nor sworn deceitfully.
He shall receive the blessing from the LORD,
  and righteousness from the God of his
  salvation (Psalm 24:3-5, KJV).

Job was unable to pray for his friends until he had repented of his sin (Job 42:6-10).

The intercessor should be motivated by a . . .

CONCERNED HEART

Not until we are ready to "put our life on the line" for those for whom we pray do we really begin to intercede. We follow the examples of Moses (Exodus 32:32), Paul (Romans 9:3; 10:1), and Jesus (Matthew 23:37; John 17; Luke 23:34).

Prepare Your Heart

1. Be still — "Be still, and know that I am God; I will be exalted among the nations, I will be exalted in the earth!" (Psalm 46:10)

2. Confess your sin — "If I regard iniquity in my heart, the Lord will not hear" (Psalm 66:18).

Praise the Lord

1. Acknowledge the presence of Jesus – "For where two or three are gathered together in My name, I am there in the midst of them" (Matthew 18:20).

2. Praise Him for the promise of prayer – "Now this is the confidence that we have in Him, that if we ask anything according to His will, He hears us. And if we know that He hears us, whatever we ask, we know that we have the petitions that we have asked of Him" (1 John 5:14,15).

PROCEDURE

A. Attendance

1. You are responsible for your hour. If you do not come or make arrangements for a replacement, the hour will be vacant.

2. If you wish to pray at a time different from your own or show someone the Prayer Chapel, enter the Chapel **on the hour only.**

B. Absence

1. If you cannot meet your hour for any reason, call your Coordinator. Give him as much notice as possible so he can find a replacement.

2. **Do not** find a replacement yourself. If you have not been assigned a Coordinator or cannot reach him, call the church office for any arrangements.

3. Contact a staff member about a replacement only in case of an emergency.

4. If you wish to change your hour, contact the church office.

C. Arrival

1. Plan to arrive at the chapel on time. Too early an arrival will disturb the Intercessor before you. Too

late will cause the chapel to be empty or the Intercessor to stay late. Be thoughtful.

2. Sign your name in the notebook on the table as you
enter. Indicate if you are a Reserve.

D. Departure

Do not leave the chapel early. You are responsible
for your entire hour. If no one comes to relieve you at
the end of your hour, wait a few minutes for a replacement before leaving.

E. Preparation

Prepare your own heart before you pray. A suggested "checklist" will be by the Rolodex.

F. The Rolodex

1. The cards will be divided into three main groups:
temporary, permanent and special. Each card will
contain a master number, date of request and the
actual request. **White** cards indicate permanent
requests which will remain on the Rolodex permanently (missionaries, churches, pastors, etc.).
Blue cards indicate temporary requests and will
remain on the Rolodex until answered (salvation,
physical healing, etc.). **Pink** cards indicate special
requests and will remain on the Rolodex **one** month
(surgery, special event, etc.).

2. Do not remove any card from the Rolodex unless
you know that the prayer has been answered or the
request is a duplicate. In either of these cases, pull
the card, note whether the card is answered or a
duplicate, sign your name with the date, and place
it in the small box marked "Rolodex cards." If the
request has been answered, write the answer and
any details that you know. Do not destroy any card.
*Be sure to sign each card so we can contact you for
information.*

3. When you finish praying, mark your place in the Rolodex with the plastic marker.

G. The Request Notebook

1. This notebook is to help keep the requests in order. Write as neatly and legibly as possible.

   When you receive a call, enter the request immediately in the notebook. Give the date and the request and as many details as possible to help others pray intelligently. Indicate if the request was phoned in. Please write your name with the request. (See sample page from REQUEST NOTEBOOK, figure 1 on page 264.)

   If you find a request which has been answered, write the information on the sheet, remove it from the notebook and put it in the ANSWER BOX.

H. Telephone Etiquette

   The telephone is the link between those with needs and the Intercessors. Your voice and manners will be the only contact some people will have with the prayer ministry.

1. Answer the phone with, "Prayer Chapel. May I help you?" Sound pleasant. Let your heart sound in your voice.

2. Keep the call brief. Make any notes that will help you enter the request.

3. If the call needs any immediate help besides prayer, refer him to a staff member.
   Note: Do not give out the name or phone number of a staff member. Ask for the caller's name and phone number, tell him you will ask a staff member to call him. Then contact a staff member and give him the information. If you need a staff member, call – but if you call, make sure you need him.

4. Ask the caller if you may lead in a brief prayer over the phone. It will take time for you to be at ease

with this practice, but God will bless it. Keep the prayer short, asking only that God's will be done.

5. If the caller wants to relay an answered prayer, enter the information in the notebook and note "Answer."

6. After each call, make a careful notation of the request in the Request Book.

7. If you make a personal request, enter it just like the others.

   This paperwork is tedious but necessary. Your careful handling of each request will insure that all the requests are placed before the Intercessors.

I. Suggestions

   1. From you: Some of the best improvements to the ministry of intercession have come from you. Please write any suggestion on a piece of paper and place it in the Answer Box.

   2. From us: You and your partner may work out any method that suits you both. Some ideas:

      (a) One reads requests while the other prays.

      (b) Sentence prayers.

      (c) One pray at a time for several requests in a row.

      (d) Let your prayers be adequate but brief.

PROBLEMS

Satan is not at all happy about the Ministry of Intercession. He will try to destroy it any way he can. Keep this in mind and pray and behave accordingly.

   1. Destruction—Pray for God's protection over the Prayer Chapel.

   2. Indifference—Pray that God will raise up enough Intercessors to fill each hour.

3. Enshrinement—Pray that we will never become more impressed with the prayer ministry than with Him.

4. Carnality—Pray that each Intercessor will keep his heart clean and committed.

5. Indiscretion—Ask God to set a guard on our mouths. Nothing will destroy the prayer ministry as quickly as careless talk about people's problems and needs. Do not share the needs with anyone except a fellow Intercessor unless you have that person's permission to do so. This matter is crucial. The effects of indiscretion are disastrous (Proverbs 16:28; 17:9; 26:20,21).

Figure 1, Sample Page From REQUEST NOTEBOOK

PRAYER REQUEST

Date of Request _____

Request:

_____

_____

_____

_____

_____

_____

_____

_____

_____

_____

_____

Request made by phone _____ Other means _____

_____

Name of person making request

_____

Phone number of person making request

_____

Figure 2, Sample of PREPARING TO PRAY card

PREPARING TO PRAY

You are about to make a difference in someone's life! You are about to pray. Get ready to see God do great things in your life and in the lives of those for whom you intercede. You have already taken the first and most important step in preparing to pray—you are here!

1. **Get comfortable**. Don't assume a physical position that is so uncomfortable you can't concentrate on the business at hand. You may pray while kneeling, standing, sitting, lying down or (as a friend of mine does) walking in circles.

2. **Be still**. "Be still, and know that I am God; I will be exalted among the nations, I will be exalted in the earth!" (Psalm 66:18). Quiet your spirit. Focus your mind.

3. **Affirm God's presence**. God Himself has invited us into His presence. Read Hebrews 4:16.

4. **Confess your sins**. "If I regard iniquity in my heart, the Lord will not hear" (Psalm 66:8). "If we confess our sins, He is faithful and just to forgive us our sins and to cleanse us from all unrighteousness" (1 John 1:9).

5. **Claim God's promises for prayer**. Read Jeremiah 33:3; Matthew 7:7,8; John 14:13,14; 1 John 5:14,15.

6. **Pray!**

Figure 3, Sample ABSENTEE CARD

Dear Intercessor,

Thank you for being a part of our church's most vital ministry, the Intercessory Prayer Ministry. I'm sorry you were not able to make your last appointment on _____.
I just wanted to remind you that we have a corp of Reserve Intercessors ready to fill in for you when you have to be absent. If you have to miss your hour, please give me a call and I'll see that your hour is filled for that day.

Signed _____

Phone Number _____

If you'd like more information regarding the use of this manual, or any other phase of an intercessory prayer ministry, please write:

LifeStyle Ministries
P. O. Box 153087
Irving, TX 75015

NOTES

Chapter Two

1. Philip Yancey, *I Was Just Wondering* (Grand Rapids: Wm. B. Eerdmans Publishing Co., 1989), p. 94.

2. *Ibid.*, p. 95.

3. D. Martyn Lloyd-Jones, *Preaching and Preachers* (Grand Rapids: Zondervan Publishing House, 1971), p. 169.

4. Barnabas Linders, *The New Century Bible, The Gospel of John* (Grand Rapids: Wm. B. Eerdmans Publishing Co., 1972), p. 475.

5. Quoted by Leon Morris, *The New International Commentary, The Gospel of John* (Grand Rapids: Wm. B. Eerdmans Publishing Co., 1971), p. 646.

6. *Ibid.*, p. 646.

7. From an interview, February 1969.

Chapter Three

1. Curtis C. Mitchell, *Praying Jesus' Way* (Old Tappan, NJ: Fleming H. Revell Company, 1977), p. 11.

2. Ernest Kasemann, *Commentary on Romans* (Grand Rapids: Wm. B. Eerdmans Publishing Co., 1980), p. 292.

Chapter Five

1. Clinton E. Arnold, *Ephesians: Power and Magic, The Concept of Power in Ephesians in Light of Its Historical Setting,* Society for New Testament Studies, Monograph Series 63 (Cambridge: Cambridge University Press, 1989), p. 15.

2. *Ibid.*, p. 14.

3. *Ibid.*, p. 116.

4. Curtis Baughan, *Ephesians* (Grand Rapids, MI: Zondervan Publishing House, 1977), p. 126.

5. Walter Wink, *Naming the Powers: The Language of Power in the New Testament,* The Powers, Vol. 1 (Philadelphia: Fortress Press, 1984), p. 85. See also Wesley Carr, *Angels and Principalities: The Background, Meaning and Development of the Pauline Phrase, Hai Archai Kai Hai Exousiai,* Society for New Testament Studies, Monograph Series 42 (Cambridge: Cambridge University Press, 1981), pp. 45-123.

6. *Ibid.,* p. 110.

7. Charles Colson, "How Prolife Protests Backfired," *Christianity Today,* Vol. 33, No. 18 (December 15, 1989), p. 82.

8. Wink, *Op. cit.,* p. 129.

9. *Ibid.,* p. 111.

Chapter Eight

1. Lewis B. Smedes, *How Can It Be All Right When Everything Is All Wrong?* (San Francisco: Harper & Row Publishers, 1982), p. 63.

2. Karl Barth, quoted by Jacobus J. Muller, *The Epistles of Paul to the Philippians and Philemon,* The New International Commentary on the New Testament (Grand Rapids: Wm. B. Eerdmans Publishing Company, 1955), p. 57.

Chapter Nine

1. Huber Drumwright, *Prayer Rediscovered* (Nashville: Broadman Press, 1978), pp. 61-63.

2. John Stott, *Involvement: Being a Responsible Christian in a Non-Christian Society* (Old Tappan, NJ: Fleming H. Revell Company, 1984), p. 105.

Chapter Ten

1. Lewis Sperry Chafer, *True Evangelism* (Findley, Ohio: The Dunham Publishing Company, 1919), pp. 3,4.

2. John Eadie, *Thessalonians: A Commentary on the Greek Text* (Grand Rapids: Baker Book House, n.d.), p. 203.

3. For a discussion of this see, *The Faith Crisis* by Ronald Dunn (Wheaton, IL: Tyndale House Publishers, 1984), pp. 63-67.

4. S. D. Gordon, *Quiet Talks on Prayer* (Old Tappan, NJ: Fleming H. Revell Company, 1967 reprint), p. 132.

Chapter Sixteen

1. C. S. Lewis, *A Grief Observed* (New York: The Seabury Press, 1963), pp. 4,5.

2. Paul Tillich, quoted by Mark Kline Taylor, *Paul Tillich, Theologian of the Boundaries* (San Francisco: Collins Liturgical Publications, 1987), p. 106.

3. Gerhard Von Rad, *Genesis* (Philadelphia: The Westminster Press, 1972), p. 322.

Chapter Nineteen

1. Harold Lindsell, *The New Paganism* (San Francisco: Harper and Row Publishers, 1987), p. x.

2. *Ibid.*, p. 213.

3. Lindsell, *Op. cit.*, p. 22.

4. George C. Findlay, *Fellowship in the Life Eternal* (Grand Rapids: Wm. B. Eerdmans Publishing Company, 1955), p. 199.

5. For a discussion of this aspect of faith see, *The Faith Crisis* by Ronald Dunn (Wheaton, IL: Tyndale House Publishers, 1984), pp. 77-87.

6. J. Edwin Orr, *The Eager Feet* (Chicago: Moody Press, 1975), p. 15.

7. J. Wesley Bready, *England: Before and After Wesley* (Seven Oaks: Hodder and Stoughton, 1939), pp. 11,14.